I0421122

Changing America 2016

2016

Our Past and Present

Timothy J. Amdahl

Copyright © 2015 Timothy J. Amdahl

All rights reserved.

ISBN:151886287X
ISBN-13:9781518862878

DEDICATION

I dedicate this book to every American. I hope this book will bring out your patriotic side that so many in our White House and our Country have lost. Let's not forget the Minute men of the past, for someday they may be called upon to return

CONTENTS

ACKNOWLEDGMENTS

This is the time for Americans and America to unite as one. This book gives you a peek at the future by taking a glimpse in the past along with what is going on currently in our media, communities, and globally. We will look at 2016 as a game changer and as a fresh start for our country by electing a new president, a new Commander in Chief, and new ideas. Come turn the pages with me as we view the Past and Present.

CHAPTER ONE

Changing America is once again ready to take on our newest challenge, electing the next president. With this obligation comes many different areas that all need to be addressed. We will look at a few of our current issues and compare them to the past. This way we can see if they have been long standing problems or if they are new and never before seen issues.

We will listen to the candidates running for president in the first Republican debate to compare how well they hold up.

We will cover all the past presidents and compare them to the current candidates. So if you are ready let's begin with a question for you. Do you know who Elizabeth Griscom is? You should that is her maiden name. She is known by most of us as Betsy Ross.

She is widely known for making the first American Flag in 1776 and instead of originally using six pointed stars went with five making it much easier.

Betsy Ross was born on a farm in West Jersey, Pennsylvania, the eighth child of seventeen, she was one of only nine that survived their childhood. In those days it was not uncommon to have lots of children.

After she had completed her schooling at a Quaker run school, her father apprenticed her to an upholsterer. At this job she fell in love with apprentice John Ross, he was the nephew of George Ross Jr., one of the signers on the Declaration of Independence.

In 1773 the couple eloped. Betsy at the age of 21 years old married John Ross at Hugg's Tavern. They opened up their own shop, and joined the Christ church. Colonel George Washington a Colonel in the Virginia Regiment, who would later become our first president often visited the church.

Betsy Ross, like I said earlier is known to have sewed the first American flag. Let's look at our flag closer and see why it has become one of our greatest symbols of freedom, strength and Democracy, and among our allies their savior.

On June 14th 1777 the Continental Congress passed the first Flag Act in order to establish an official flag for our new nation. The flag was to have 13 stripes alternating in Red and White, along with 13 White stars in a field of Blue representing the constellation. Congress passed several acts throughout the years that changed the look and design of the flag. Let's look at some of those acts.

Act of January 13, 1794 - provided for 15 stripes and 15 stars after May 1795.

Act of April 4, 1818 - provided for 13 stripes and one star for each State, to be added to the flag on the 4th of July following the admission of each new State, signed by President Monroe.

Executive Order of President Taft dated June 24, 1912 - established proportions of the flag and provided for arrangement of the stars in six horizontal rows of eight each, a single point of each star to be upward.

Executive Order of President Eisenhower dated January 3, 1959 - provided for the arrangement of the stars in seven rows of seven stars each, staggered horizontally and vertically.

Executive Order of President Eisenhower dated August 21, 1959 - provided for the arrangement of the stars in nine rows of stars staggered horizontally and eleven rows of stars staggered vertically.

There was the Grand Union Flag, Betsy Ross Flag, 13 Star Flag, 15 Star Flag, Civil War 35 Star Flag, and Old Glory, as well as the Don't tread on me flag. There are many other designs that are out there from the earlier years. Today we all use a uniformed flag pattern. The colors too have been said to have different meanings, George Washington was said to have used red for the British, others had said red was for blood and courage.

blue was to represent the sky and white for purity. As you can see, even the flag has had to change with the times.

Let's look and see if there were conflicts with our flag back in the early years, or even now.

Back in **1903** the case of **Halter VS. Nebraska** made it a crime to sell or to possess anything printed or placed for the purpose of advertising the representation of the United States Flag. Many of the States had their own laws in regards to desecrating the flag. Images of the flag in books and magazines were exempt.

Halter, owner of a bottling company was charged with selling beer bottles with the American Flag on the label. He never argued that the law violated his First Amendment, the right to freedom of speech.

The Supreme Court ruled 8 to 1 that the States do have the authority to ban desecration of the American Flag, also ruling advertisement can be categorized as desecration.

In a more recent case posted in the news on September of 2014 The 9th U.S. Circuit Court of Appeals refused to listen to the parents, Republican lawmakers, and conservative groups. They were requesting a rehearing of a case giving South Bay High School the right to order students wearing the American Flag, adorning shirts to wear them inside out during the Cinco-de-Mayo celebration.

Just to clarify this the word adorn means to make beautiful, or attractive.

On this note by itself, is a violation of the Flag laws which states the Flag is to be flown freely and not pulled back.

Here the flag is being flown in reverse inside an Americans shirt. Tell me where is the beauty in that? This is one of the most disgraceful acts that can be done. No flag is to fly higher or above ours period.

Their reasoning is due to the hostility and history between the Latino and Whites, and fear of threats of aggression during the Cinco-de-Mayo celebration. William Becker the lawyer for the parents is vowing to take this to the Supreme Court.

Let's look at the do's and don'ts of the American Flag. When two or more Flags are flown or displayed of other nationalities, they are to be flown on separate staffs and at the same height and size, with neither being above the other in time of peace. International usage forbids one flag to fly above another in time of peace. So why do our Courts force us to lower our flag during the time of Cinco-de-Mayo?

The Flag should never be dipped to any person or thing, unless it is the ensign responding to a ship of a foreign nation.

The flag should never be flown upside down except in case of danger to life or property.

The flag should not be worn as clothing apparel or as drapery. It should not be used to cover a speaker's desk. Bunting of Blue, White, and Red can be used for this making sure the Blue is on top.

The flag is not to be drawn back or bunched up in any way.

The flag should never be used as a covering for a ceiling.

The flag should never be used for any advertising purposes. It should not be embroidered, printed, or otherwise impressed on such articles as cushions, handkerchiefs, napkins, boxes, or anything that is to be thought of as temporary use.

The flag should never be fastened, displayed, used or stored in a manner that permits it to be easily soiled, torn, or damaged.

The flag is not to be used as part of a costume, or athletic uniform, with the exception of a flag patch may be used on a uniform of either military, fireman, or police officers, and members of a patriotic organization.

Flag lapel pins may also be worn and are to be worn near the heart.

The flag should never have any mark, insignia, letter, word, number, figure, or drawing placed on it, or attached to it of any kind.

The flag should never be used as a receptacle for, receiving, holding, carrying, or delivering anything.

The flag should never be stepped on.

Let's look at some more cases. In the case we just looked at the word that seemed to make the Judge's decision was **political correctness**.

In Virginia Beach there is the story of Vanessa Hicks. A mother who posted a picture of her son cradled in an American Flag being held by his father who was in the Navy. The baby was only eight days old. She had received a lot of heat for posting the picture stating she was unpatriotic and was desecrating the flag.

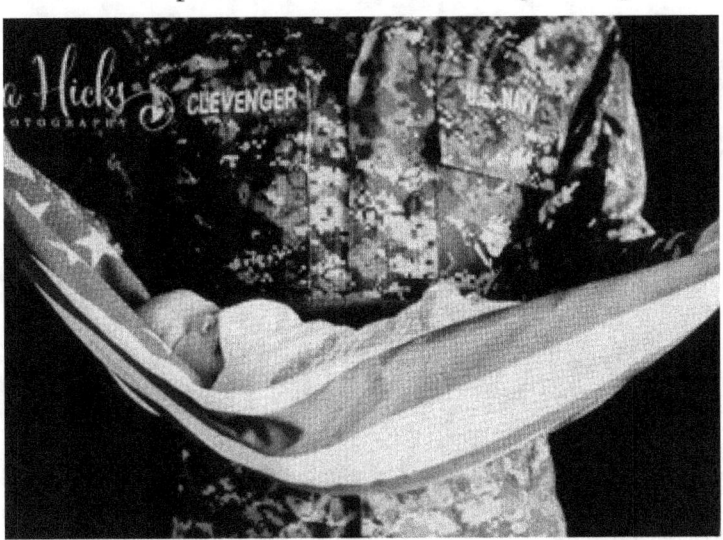

Her response was that she was not dishonoring or disrespecting the flag code.

Let's look at the violations.

The flag should not be worn as clothing apparel or as drapery. It should not be used to cover a speaker's desk. The child appears draped.

The flag is not to be drawn back or bunched up in any way. Looks bunched up on the ends to me.

The flag is not to be used as part of a costume, or athletic uniform, except a flag patch may be used on a uniform of either military, fireman, or police officers, and members of a patriotic organization.

The flag should never be used as a receptacle for, **receiving**, **holding, carrying**, or **delivering anything**. The flag appears to be carrying a baby.

If not for the purpose of presentation, it becomes part of the costume of the baby.

While I do believe she meant only patriotic pride and honor, and at no time meant to purposely disrespect the flag, I do believe she did violate the Flag Code. Do I think she should be punished absolutely not. This is about learning about our flag and honoring it. They are serving in one of our branches of military. Is this not a great lesson for us all to unite and remember what the Flag stands for. Freedom to express one's self. Sure she, as well as the rest of us can learn from this. I knew very little myself on the do's and don'ts till I searched for more information.

We should use this as a tool to bring Americans together. To unite and show our flag with pride and do it under the guidelines that the code stipulates.

A Cape Coral business could face fines for displaying dozens of American Flags. A code enforcement officer has stated that the flags being flown outside the Family Hardware business are violating city code.

Jeff Verzi said each flag has meaning as he describes each representing someone close to him. He stated he was not trying to be disrespectful to the city.

According to the city ordinance, it's against city code for any sign or banner to be placed in the right of way. City officials said it is mainly for safety purposes.

Again the American Flag comes under attack as someone tries to show their patriotism. Are we missing something here is there any way we could see to it this owner's flags could be flown and still not violate the city code? Is this someone who is just looking to see if he can push his American right to free speech?

What if they set up an area for all to fly flags? Each person could be responsible for their own flag and pole. I have seen them do this in areas for Christmas trees, why not flags? The other argument is, is a flag a banner or a sign? We can fight over minute technicalities, or we can look at solving problems with solutions. Is it better to be right or United? Do we fight to better America? There are more cases, let's keep going.

We have to look at both the freedom of expression and the desecration of the flag when it comes to burning our flag.

United States VS, Eichman consolidated two cases together where persons were prosecuted for violating the Flag protection Act of 1989. This acts states the following.

Whoever knowingly mutilates, defaces, physically defiles, burns, maintains on the floor or ground, or tramples upon any flag of the United States shall be fined under this title or imprisoned for not more than one year, or both. This subsection does not prohibit any conduct consisting of the disposal of a flag when it has become worn or soiled.

In an earlier case Texas VS. Johnson the Supreme Court ruled in favor of Johnson who argued his rights were violated to his freedom of speech.

At what point do we say yes you have rights but with those rights come consequences. The person who wishes to protest burning the flag is going beyond his right to free speech. The flag is sacred to us who have served in the military and to all those who have given their lives for our country. They can argue they have the right to free speech, but what is the difference between that, and someone yelling fire in a crowded area? There is none. Burn a flag on a military installation in protest and tell me what happens to the protester.

Are these people who wish to demonstrate, only able to do so with fire? Why destroy the flag that represents America and the very voices these people wish to express to and for? Do these people not see themselves as haters of America? They are no better than those that loot and destroy a community to voice their opinion, Ferguson, Baltimore.

There was Smith VS. Goguen where it had nothing to do with protest but where the flag was displayed, which was on the seat of Smith's pants. He was convicted and given a 6 month prison sentence and the case went to the Supreme Court where they said the law was too vague. They did say had it been an earlier era that he could have been found guilty, but due to the changing and the diversity what one sees as desecrating another might not.

In Texas we have the battle of heights between the United States Flag and the Flag of Texas.

In the Texas Government Code, Chapter 3100, Subchapter A, Sec. 3100.055(b), titled: Display on Flagpole/Flagstaff with Flag of the United States, the code reads:

"If the state flag and the flag of the United States are displayed on flagpoles/flagstaffs at the same location: (1) the flags should be displayed on flagpoles/flagstaffs of the same height."

I know that no flag should fly higher than that of the United States Flag. And it should be raised before all others. Let's move on to those that wish to express themselves by stomping on the American Flag.

In Ferguson, Missouri, a reporter named Rick Jenkins reported a disturbance in Ferguson. It was on the Kelly file as they show it on someone's cell phone being videoed. A Vietnam Veteran questions a couple Black men on why they are stomping on the flag. Their response, "It's what your flag represents doing to us."

I think it shows that no matter what people feel, through using the flag they will be heard better. Maybe if we can educate them on speaking their mind while holding the flag they will be heard better. What is it that makes our flag such a spokesman for everybody? Let's look at where our flag has been.

July 4,1675- August 12,1676 King Phillips War. The Wampanoag nation was on friendly terms with the settlers and Colonists. However Metacom, nicknamed King Phillip by the Colonists, led the New England Native Americans to fight against the Colonists, as they seized more and more land. The New England Confederation was key in their success to victory over the Native Americans. Those involved were the New England Colonies vs. Wampanoag, Narragansett, and Nipmuck Indians.

1689-1697 was the Kings **Williams War** it lasted eight years it was between the English Colonies and France.

Now you can see how war has been around a long time, but let's bring it up to the **Revolutionary War in 1775**. The English Colonists battle Great Britain.

The battle between the United 13 Colonies and Great Britain. Americans felt they deserved all the rights of Englishmen. The British, on the other hand, felt that the colonies were created to be used in the way that best suited the crown and parliament. This conflict is embodied in one of the rallying cries of the American Revolution: **No Taxation Without Representation**.

The Colonial Legislators signified in many ways that the Colonies were independent. The Legislators were allowed to levy taxes and muster troops, along with pass laws.

In 1798-1800, was the **Franco American Naval War**, between France and United States.

In 1801-1805, and 1815 there was the **Barbary Wars**, these wars consisted of the United States vs. Morocco, Algiers, Tunis, and Tripoli.

1812-1815, consisted of the **War of 1812**. The United States vs. Great Britain.

1813-1814, was the **Creek War** involving the United States vs. Creek Indians.

In 1836, was the **War of Texas Independence.** This was where Texas battled Mexico. Let's look at this war closer on April 6, 1830 Mexican government forbids further Americans from migrating to Texas which was under Mexico control. Mexican Government was dictating all the policies.

To me this is interesting that now we are having to turn things around and stop the Mexicans from migrating to the United States illegally.

On October 2, the Battle of Gonzales is waged and the **War of Texas Independence** begins.
On October 9, the Battle of Goliad takes place and ends with a victory for Texas.
On October 28, Texans are victorious at the Battle of Concepcion despite being outnumbered 5 to 1.
On December 11, the Siege of Bexar ends with the Texans capturing San Antonio.

1846-1848 was the **Mexican American War** between the United States and Mexico.

1861-1865 was the infamous **Civil War** between the Confederate and the Union. This was a war between the North and the south. Slavery was a part of the reason for the Civil War but the other reasons were due to taxation, tariffs, internal improvements, and the military. Today the Confederate flag too has been soiled by ignorance labeling the flag as racist. If the South would have won the United States flag could have easily taken its spot.

There has been many more wars and we have lost many great soldiers as they fought for our freedom. We owe it to them to show them the respect that they all deserve when it comes to holding, caring, and speaking with our great flag. We owe it to our citizens and our children as we are teaching and educating through our own actions. When we hold the flag, we are holding our country, just like when we salute her.

Let us move on to another area that seems to be a big issue today, which also started back in the days of the Civil War, and before. Slavery was a big issue back then and it has continued in today's society to still linger heavily.

So let us look at it and see if we can learn anything from this travesty. One thing we have to take into consideration is the time. Many of the people of today namely Whites, do not look at the Blacks as they did back then, yet they are constantly being blamed for the fall of the Blackman. Why? Is there a reason? Let's explore as we travel back through time.

In 1619 at Jamestown, Va. Approximately 20 Africans are sold into slavery in the British North American Colonies.

The Dutch West India Company imported 11 Black male slaves into the New Netherlands in 1626. In 1636 the Colonial North American Trade begins, when the first American slave carrier named **Desire** is built and launched in Massachusetts.

In 1641 Massachusetts is the first State to legalize slavery.

In 1662 Virginia enacts a law of hereditary slavery, which meant the child born of an enslaved mother inherits her slave status.

In 1676 Black slaves and Black and White indentured servants united together to participate in the Bacons Rebellion.

In 1680 The State of Virginia did not allow Blacks and slaves to bear arms, or gather in large crowds.

In 1682 Virginia declares that all imported Black servants are slaves for life.

In 1684 New York makes it illegal for slaves to sell goods

In 1691 Virginia passes a law forbidding Whites to marry Blacks, or Natives Americans. South Carolina passes the first comprehensive slave codes.

In 1700 Pennsylvania legalizes slavery.

In 1702 New York passes an act regulating slaves on meetings of three or more slaves, trading by slaves, as well as testimony of slaves in court.

In 1703 Massachusetts requires every master who liberates a slave to pay a bond of 50 pounds or more in case the freedman becomes a public charge. Connecticut also punished by whipping the slaves who disturbed the peace, or assaulted White persons. Rhode Island made it illegal for Blacks and Indians to be out at night without a pass.

We have covered near one hundred years let's look at the next hundred years and see how life changes or remains the same. Are you ready to travel onwards? We will be coming back to this era shortly.

In 1776 the declaration of independence was signed. During this year in Pennsylvania the Society of Friends also known as Quakers, forbid their members from holding slaves, and Delaware prohibits importation of slaves.

In 1777 Vermont is the first of the thirteen colonies to abolish slavery. They also gave all adult males the right to vote. In New York they gave the right to vote to all free propertied men regardless of color and their prior servitude.

In 1778 Rhode Island forbid the removal from slaves from the State. Virginia prohibits importation of slaves.

In 1780 two years later Delaware makes it illegal to enslave imported Africans. Pennsylvania begins emancipation gradually.

In 1783 Virginia emancipates those slaves that served in the colonial forces against Britain, provided their masters give them permission. In the next three years emancipation begins with Rhode Island, Connecticut, North Carolina and New York.

In 1785 Virginia deems any person with black blood to be a Mulatto and terms the use of the word Negro to be understood to include them.

In 1787 Richard Allen a Black preacher becomes the founder of the African Methodist Episcopal church in Philadelphia, Pennsylvania. South Carolina ends domestic and international slave trade.

In 1793 The first fugitive State law is passed, giving slave owners permission to pursue the slave fugitives across State line, and a penal offense to those who encourage runaway slaves.

In 1800 Congress prohibits U.S. citizens from exporting slaves.

In 1801 Congress extends the Virginia, and Maryland slavery laws into the district of Columbia, establishing a federally authorized slave code.

In 1803 South Carolina opens a new port to accommodate the importation of African slaves.

In 1804 The U.S. prohibits the importation of slaves from foreign territories into Louisiana.

Let's just take a minute and review what we have so far. To me there is a lot of push, pull, push. I think one State becomes strict and legalizes slavery then another State gives leniency and goes the other direction and Congress is like the thread that weaves these States and their laws and guidelines together, but in doing so there is a lot of back and forth. At this point I can see why the African American community has been so against the Whites. Now having said that, remember the times as we continue to drive forwards and look at this from all angles. This is not being reviewed to point out blame, it is being reviewed to bring closer and Americans together as one united family. This is what Changing America's books are about. If you are ready we will move on in to the 1800's as we work our way closer and closer from history to today's reality.

In 1874 The Democrats win control of both Houses of Congress for the first time since the Antebellum years. The Whites regain control of the South Carolina Legislature.

In 1875 a Republican Congress passes a Civil Rights Act granting African Americans equal access to public accommodations, including transportation.

In 1902 Harry (Bucky) Lew was the first African American to breach the color line in professional basketball.

In 1914 Fred Faulcon as Scoutmaster organized the integrated Boy Scout troop 7.

In 1918 African American troops fought in segregated units in World War I. The 360th Regiment served longer in combat than any other unit. The Germans called them the Hell Fighters.

The National Association for colored people (NAACP) formed a Chapter by Harold M. Wingood.

In 1920 the Ku Klux Klan resurfaced after laying dormant. They had over 2 million supporters back in those days. The 19th Amendment gave women the right to vote.

In 1927 the Model A was introduced by Henry Ford. America was on its way to becoming bigger and better, but there were still many rough roads ahead for the African American communities.

In 1937 Joe Lewis won the world heavyweight boxing title.

In 1951 racial segregation in Washington D.C. restaurants is declared unconstitutional by the U.S. supreme Court. During this time approximately 3500 Whites try and keep an African American family from moving into an apartment building in Cicero.

In 1952 The Tuskegee Institute reports that there has been no reported lynching's in more than 70 years in the United States.

In 1953 African American residents in Baton Rouge establish a boycott of the city's segregated transportation system, during this same time Willie Thrower joins the Chicago Bears and becomes the first African American NFL quarterback.

In 1954 there is the Brown VS. Board of Education case it involved African American children in Topeka, Kansas, who were being denied the right to go to an all white school. Stating separate but equal with the 1896 ruling in Plessy VS. Ferguson, which gave legal standing to separate but equal. This doctrine stipulated that any facility had to be equal in standings and quality. In the Brown VS. Board of Education they argued that they were not equal. The 14th Amendment was used to show separate facilities based on race were not equal. The NAACP went to argue and the Supreme Court ruled in the Browns favor. Allowing Blacks to go to an all white school.

In the same year Malcolm X becomes Minister of Islam No.7 in New York City.

In 1955 Rosa Parks is arrested after refusing to give up her seat on a bus to a white person in Montgomery, Alabama. Martin Luther King Jr. is elected President of the Montgomery Improvement Association.

In 1956 Nat King Cole becomes the first African American to host a prime time show on national television.

In 1957 Dorothy Irene Height is elected President of the National Council of Negro Women.

We are 58 years away from being caught up to the present time. I am 53 years old so this is near my time, so let's look at this era and see how there are two sides to every debate.

In today's world we see many more prominent blacks. There are Doctors, Lawyers, Teachers, Business owners, Real estate agents, even the President of the United States. President Obama in 2012 signed an Executive Order on Educational Excellence for African Americans. Education has always been an area of concern when it came to equality.

They look at statistics that show black children are far below in graduating high school. What they don't say is that these schools are full of gangs and kids that have grown up with only one parent.

Most of their influence is from the thugs on the streets who are making fast money, riding around in a fancy car. Is the White man to blame for the kids that are out there selling drugs?

If these kids dads were not in jail and were not out with other women trying to be players, would these kids have a different outlook on life? Would these communities that are mostly black have a better chance if the dads were in the home instead of jail?

We have seen what history has done to them through no fault of their own, but it is like comparing a woman who has been raped and chooses to stay a victim. They too appear to wish to stay victims of their ancestors travesties.

Today they can go to better schools if they are willing to leave their run down depleted schools that teachers fear to teach at. They can go out and get jobs now in many cases easier than others due to many places have to hire so many of different racial or sexual genders.

If they wish to build their communities together they can do that as well. We have seen them come together for all the wrong reasons and demonstrate in all the wrong ways. Communities are built by helping each other not by dividing Blacks against the whites, Poor against the police. Gangs can be controlled through the same crowds that were there rallying for Michael Brown who was a criminal at the time when he resisted and threatened the officer.

There are leaders that seem to only like creating factions keeping the black man down, whether on purpose or through their own ignorance I'm not sure. Look at Al Sharpton, Barrack Obama, and many more that seem to ignore everything not speaking at all in regards to peace and justice.

Where is Opra Winfrey? She could be very influential, everyone used to look up to her. What about Rihanna or Nicki Minaj. In today's world singers are looked up to as other celebrities.

I understand that healing takes time but where is the thanks to the White Man who stood among the Blacks trying to rid slavery and bring equality? The blacks want to move forwards while still continuing to harbor hatred toward the white male for what has happened hundreds of years ago. They have Black History month, We do not have White History Month. We celebrate Martin Luther King Jr. day. Which is a good thing, but Martin Luther King wanted these children to get a better education so why do the communities not try to rid the school of the gangs and violence that infests their schools and communities?

They have BETV, (Black Entertainment TV). We would be labeled racist if we had WETV, (White Entertainment TV). They have all Black Colleges out there promoting segregation while crying equality. You will not see any all white schools out there, in fact we just got done going through the history getting rid of segregation. Blacks do get to vote now as do women. America has come a long ways. We do not see blacks being whipped, or hung like in the old days.

23

Yes we do still see them getting shot, stabbed, assaulting others, robbing, destroying, looting, and tearing down their own communities as they protest unfairness and equality. Most these things happen as they do it to themselves black on black gang activities.

I am not sure how fair it is to the businesses they rob and loot. I am not prejudice I do not judge a man by his color I judge them by their character. I believe that equal means equal They destroyed Ferguson and Baltimore, and Baltimore was being run by black leaders, so there was no one to blame other than the black leaders.

While I said earlier it is not about blaming, but understanding so that we can fix these issues and move forwards. The Confederate Flag is being attacked without prejudice as they try to connect it to racism, but the fact is it is a part of our history. Removing the flag from existence, is like tearing out a hundred years of history from the history books. This flag offends them, sorry it is a part of our history good or bad. We have come a long ways since then. They want the Confederate flag gone, yet they trample on and burn the American flag which is the flag that helped get them their freedom.

They need to decide whether they want help or if they want blame, because racism is not just whites against blacks, but blacks against whites. And the people of today are not the people of yesterday. We need our leaders Al Sharpton and President Obama to lead the black culture so they can prosper, instead of enable and promote hatred and violence.

CHAPTER TWO

This next chapter, we will look at one of the big topics in America, immigration. This is an area that the next President of the United States will have to address.

The settling of America began with 102 English Colonists, who joined together to govern themselves. They were known as the Pilgrims. In 1620 they set sail on the famous ship the Mayflower and landed in Plymouth, Massachusetts. This is considered to be the start of the European migration. 18 years later after the Mayflowers arrival, the Swedes begin to migrate to America.

The Swedes were an organized group sent by their government to establish a Colony in Delaware. In 1655 the Colony was lost to the Dutch.

In the mid 1840's the Swedish farmers had started to migrate out East, to New York and continued through World War I. Many came from Germany and Ireland, but they came from Netherlands, Spain, Italy, Scandinavian countries, and Eastern Europe as well. America was a mixture of many different ethnic groups, with diverse cultural and religious beliefs and practices.

The Naturalization Act of 1790 stipulated that any alien being a free white person, may be admitted to become a citizen of the United States.

In 1875 the Supreme Court declared that U.S. Immigration is the responsibility of the Federal Government.

In 1882 the Chinese Exclusion Act, prohibited certain laborers from immigrating to the United States.

In 1885-1887 Alien Contract Labor Laws prohibited certain laborers from immigrating to the United States.

In 1891 the Federal Government took over the responsibilities of inspecting, admitting, rejecting, and processing all immigrants seeking admission in to the United States.

On January 2, 1892 a new U.S. Immigration Station opened up on Ellis Island in New York Harbor.

In 1903 the Act that restated the 1891 provisions called for rules to cover the entry and inspections of aliens crossing the Mexican border

In 1907 The U.S. Immigration Act of 1907 reorganized the States bordering Mexico, which were (Arizona, New Mexico, and a large part of Texas) into Mexican border districts to help maintain custody and control of the immigrants entering the United States.

Between the years of 1917 and 1924 a series of laws were passed further limiting the immigration in to the United States, using a quota system and issuing passport requirements. They expanded the category of excludable aliens to include all Asians except Japanese.

The 1924 Act reduced the number of U.S. Immigration Visas, which they distributed according to national origin.

The Alien Registration Act of 1940 required all aliens (none U.S. Citizens) within the United States to register with the government and receive a alien registration receipt card, later to be switched in 1950 for the Green Card, Form I-151.

The 1952 Act established the current day U.S. Immigration system. It created a quota system which imposed limits on a per country basis. It also established the preference system giving priority to those family members and persons with skills.

The 1968 Act eliminated U.S. Immigration discrimination based on race, sex, place of birth, and residence it also officially abolished restrictions on Oriental U.S. Immigration.

The 1976 Act eliminated preferential treatment for residents in the Western Hemisphere.

The 1986 Act focused on reducing illegal U.S. Immigration. It legalized hundreds of thousands of illegal's, known as the 1986 Immigration Amnesty.

It introduced the employers sanctions program, fining anybody that hires illegal aliens. It also passed tough marriage laws regarding illegal immigrants.

The 1990 Act established an annual limit for certain categories of immigrants. It was aimed at bringing in certain type immigrants with special skills. They were looking for those that could contribute to this country through financial, education, or professionally.

There is also the U.S. Patriot Act of 2001 uniting, and strengthening America, by providing the necessary tools needed to stop and intervene on terrorism.

America has come a long ways but it has treated immigration as a big brother or a friend. We need to be the parents of our own country as we learn to tell people No at times. This is an area that is long overdue to be held accountable. The Democrats want to bring in immigrants to add to their voter numbers. It was the same way with slavery back in the old days. The democrats wished to control and hold a certain number of slaves so as to increase their odds on winning elections.

Today we will be looking at these Presidential candidates to see how they think it should be addressed. Don't let Obama say we do not have a problem, or to look the other way as he has done on so very many issues. If they are illegal's than they have not sworn allegiance to our country, or our countrymen. Home Land Security has told the border patrol to slow down. Why? Maybe if they capture less illegal's it will look like the numbers are declining.

Illegal's are coming.

How will America welcome them?

By land or by water they will try to enter the United States. There is one Presidential Candidate that was the first to bring this long term problem to America's attention, yes it was Donald Trump. Yes he took a lot of flack as he stood strong on his principles and America's as well.

Donald Trump has no problem with those that are legal only those that are illegal, who wish to rob, rape, and steal. Those that wish to work for low wages and pay no taxes. Those that run to the emergency room for the sniffles and let us tax payers pay for it.

One of the areas that is being talked about by Donald Trump is the removing of all illegal citizens. This area has come under debate by the 14th Amendment, under the citizenship clause which states.

"All persons born or naturalized in the United States, and subject to the jurisdiction thereof, are citizens of the United States and of the State wherein they reside."

The Fourteenth Amendment does not provide any procedure for revocation of United States citizenship. Under the Supreme Court precedent of **Afroyim v. Rusk**, loss of 14th-Amendment-based U.S. citizenship is possible only under the following circumstances:

> **Fraud in the naturalization process**. Technically this is not loss of citizenship, but rather a voiding of the purported naturalization and a declaration that the immigrant *never was* a U.S. citizen.

Is it not a crime to enter this country illegally? Do they not enter for the sole purpose of obtaining a citizenship status? Americans want action, we want results. What has President Obama done besides turn a blind eye along with Hillary Clinton looking to gain Hispanic votes.

It is time we take our country back. We need a president that will not only address these issues, but take action to see it done. Donald Trump openly stated his opinion. Most the Presidential Candidates tiptoed around this issue, hesitant to make a stand fearing to lose valuable votes. Let me rephrase that, fearing to lose a mass of votes from those that don't contribute to our society, illegal immigrants.

Listen to these candidates as they speak to America. Are they speaking in a manner that their words can be interpreted in more than one way? Are they speaking to everyone the same or do they try to speak a little differently to the Swing States. Those are the States that can be swayed to either candidate depending on how they feel the candidate will best represent them.

The States that appear to be strong Swing States are Florida, Ohio, and Missouri. Ohio and Missouri were ranked 19th, and Florida was ranked 22nd as below poverty level in the United States from the time I did my first book. Some of the other states that have been mentioned as possible Swing States were Virginia, North Carolina, Nevada, New Mexico, Indiana, and Michigan.

We will just have to watch and see if there is any validity to this. Let's look at a few of the Presidential candidates from my last book as we will cover more of them throughout this book. I am going to start with one I do not like personally. Hillary Clinton is doing everything I have been talking about, trying to reach everyone without saying anything. As you can see in her short campaign add.

Hillary R Clinton's Campaign ad

Hillary R. Clinton the former Secretary of State ran a two minute eighteen second campaign add. She told the world she was running for president.

The ad depicted a lady getting her garden started; it showed a mother moving with her child to a better school. It showed foreigners starting their own business and a mother rejoining the work force after five years as a stay at home mother with her child.

It showed a young black couple, the woman pregnant. There was an oriental applying for a job, as she mentioned what the real world was like after college. The ad showed two gay guys holding hands, a young black boy in a school play. There was an older white lady talking about retirement and a couple that were racially mixed. It ended with them talking about the fifth generation of a business and cats and dogs strategically placed within the ad of her campaign message.

Let us look at what the ad was saying and who it's targeting. It targets both stay at home moms and working moms. It targets the single moms that are getting a new start in a new school. It targets all the foreigners, both legal and illegal immigrants directly and indirectly. It targets the women who want to get back to work after being home with their kids for years. It targets the blacks from a young boy in school to a pregnant black woman. It targets the gays as you see two guys holding hands. They mention fifth generation workers as a strong family bond. They showed pets to appeal to the pet lovers.

Senator Rand Paul Campaign speech

Senator Rand Paul announces his running for office as he gives his speech. Here is his rally for president.

"I have a message, a message that is loud and clear and does not mince words. We have come to take our country back. **We have come to take our country back** from the special interests that use Washington as their personal piggy bank. The special interests that are more concerned with their welfare then the general welfare. The Washington machine that gobbles up our freedom and invades every nook and cranny of our lives must be stopped."

"Less than five years ago I stood down the road in my home town and said those same words. I wasn't supposed to win, no one thought I would. Some people ask me then why are you running? The answer is the same now as it was then; I have a vision for America. I want to be a part of a return to prosperity, a true economic boom that lifts all Americans. **A government restrained by the constitution,** A return to privacy, opportunity, liberty. Too often when the republicans have won we have squandered our victory by becoming part of the Washington machine. **That's not who I am**. That's not why I ran for office a few years ago. The truth is I love my life as a small town doctor. Every day I woke up and felt lucky I was able to do the things I love. More importantly I was able to do the things that made a difference in people's lives. I never could have done any of this without the help of my parents who are here today.

I'd like you to join me and thank my mother and dad.

With my parents help I was able to make it through long years of medical training to become an eye surgeon. For me, there is nothing that compares to helping someone see well.

Last august I was privileged to have traveled to Guatemala on a medical mission trip, together with a team of surgeons we operated on more than two hundred people that were blind or nearly blind from cataracts. I was grateful to be able to put my scrubs back on peer into the oculars and microscope and focus on the task at hand, to take a surgical approach to fix a problem.

One day a man arrives in Guatemala and told me I had operated on his wife the day before. His wife could see clearly for the first time in years. She had begged him to get on the bus to travel the winding roads and come back to our surgical center he too was nearly blind from cataracts. After his surgery the next day his wife set next to me as I unveiled the patch from his eyes there was a powerful emotional moment for me to see them looking at each other clearly for the first time in years. To see the face they loved again. As I saw the joy in their eyes I thought to myself this is why I became a doctor. In that moment I also remembered my grandmother who inspired me to become an eye surgeon.

She spent hours with me as a kid, we would sort through her old coin collections looking for wheat pennies and Indian heads, but as her vision began to fail, I became her eyes, to inspect the faintness of the mint marks on the weathered old coins.

I went to the Ophthalmologist when she had her corneas replaced. I was also with her when she got the news that macular degeneration had done irreparable harm.

My hope to make my grandmother see again made me want to become an eye surgeon to make a difference in people's lives. I've been fortunate to live the American dream. I worry that the opportunity and hope are slipping away for our sons and daughters. As I watch our great economy collapse under mounting spending and debt,

I think what kind of America will our grand children see? It seems to me both parties and the entire political system are to blame. Big government debt doubled under the republican administration and it's now tripling under Barrack Obama's watch. President Obama is on course to add more debt than all of the previous presidents combined. We borrow a million dollars a minute. This vast accumulation of debt not just threatens our economy, but our security.

We can wake up now and do the right thing, quit spending money we don't have. This message of liberty is for all Americans, from all walks of life. The message of Liberty, opportunity and justice, this is for all Americans whether you wear a suit, uniform, or overalls, whether you're White, Black, rich, or poor In order to restore America one thing is for sure, we must not dilute our message or give up on our principles. If we nominate a candidate that is simply democrat like, what's the point?

We need to boldly proclaim our vision for America. We need to go forth under the banner of liberty that clutches the constitution in one hand and the Bill of Rights in the other. Washington is horribly broken I fear it can't be fixed from within. We the people must wise up and demand action. Congress will never balance the budget unless you force them to do so. Congress has abysmal record with balancing anything. Our only recall is to force congress to balance the budget with a constitutional amendment. I have been to Washington and let me tell you there is no monopoly on knowledge there. I ran for office there because **we have too many career politicians.**

I believe it is more important now than ever before, we limit the president to two terms. It is about time we limit the terms of Congress. I want to reform Washington. I want common sense rules that will break the log jamming congress. That's why I've introduced a **Read the Bills act**. The bill is put on our desk with only a few hours before a vote, so I proposed something truly extraordinary. Let's read the Bills every page. From the time I was a very young boy I was taught to love and appreciate America. Love of liberty pulses in my veins, not because we have beautiful mountains and white sand beaches, although we do and not because we have an abundance of resources, it's more visceral than that.

Our great Nation was founded on the extraordinary notion government should be restrained and freedom should be maximized. America is to me is that beacon. We are unique among nations because our country stands for freedom. Freedom nurtured from a rebellious group of colonies into the world's greatest nation.

When tyranny threatened the world America lead the way to rid the world of Nazis, fascist regimes. Resolutely we stood decade after decade against communism, the engine of capitalism to finally win over the sputtering, incompetence of socialism. We won the cold war. American freedom is so intertwined that people are dying trying to get here.

The freedom we have fostered here in America has unleashed genius in advancement like never before. Yet our great nation still needs new ideas and answers to old problems. From an early age I worked. I taught swimming lessons, I mowed lawns, I did landscaping I put roofs on houses, I painted houses. I never saw work though as punishment. Work always gave me a sense of who I am. Self-esteem can't be given it must be earned. Work is not punishment, work is the reward.

Two of my sons work minimum wage jobs while they go to college. I am proud of them as I see them realize the value of hard work. I can see their self-esteem grow as they cash their paychecks. I have a vision for America everyone that wants to work will have a job. Many Americans that were being left behind, the reward of work seemed beyond their grasp. Under the watch of both parties, the poor seem to get poorer and the rich seem to get richer. Trillion dollar government stimulus packages have only widened the income gap. Politically correct cronies get tax payer dollars by the hundreds of millions and poor people across America continue to suffer. I have a different vision an ambitious vision, a vision that will offer opportunity to all Americans, especially those who had been left behind.

My plan, my plan includes economic freedom zones to allow improvised areas like Detroit, West Lovell and Eastern Kentucky to prosper by leaving more money in the pockets of the people that live there. Can you imagine what a billion dollar stimulus could do for Detroit?

I am convinced most Americans want to work. I want to free up the great engine of American prosperity, I want to see millions of Americans back at work. In my vision for America we'll bring back manufacturing jobs that pay well. We, will dramatically lower the tax on American companies that wish to bring their profits home. More than two trillion dollars in American profit currently sits overseas. In my vision new highways and bridges will be built across the country not by raising taxes but by lowering the taxes to bring this American profit home. Even in this polarized congress we have a chance at passing this. I say let's bring home two trillion dollars to America, **let's bring it home now.**

Liberal policies have failed our inner cities; let's just get the facts straight, they have failed our inner cities. Our schools are not equal and our poverty gap continues to widen. Martin Luther King spoke of two Americas. He described them as two starkly different Americas that exist side by side.

In one America people experienced the opportunity of life, liberty and the pursuit of happiness. In the other America people experienced a daily ugliness dashed hopes and leaves only fatigue of despair. Although I was born into the America that experiences and believes in opportunity. My trips to Detroit and Chicago have revealed an undercurrent of unease.

It's time for a new way, predicated on justice opportunity and freedom. Those of us who have enjoyed the American dream must break down the wall that separates us from the other America. I want all our children to have the same opportunity that I had. We need to stop limiting kids in poor neighborhoods, failing in public schools and offer them school choice. It won't happen though unless we realize we can't borrow our way to prosperity.

Currently three trillion dollars comes in to the department of treasury, couldn't we just survive on three trillion dollars? Let's do something extraordinary **let's just spend what comes in.** In my vision of America, freedom and prosperity can only be achieved against enemies dead set on attacking us. Without question we must defend ourselves and American interests from our enemies, but **until we name the enemy we can't win the war** . The enemy is Radical Islam, you can't get around it. Not only will I name the enemy I will do whatever it takes to defend America from these haters of mankind. We need a national defense robust enough to defend against all attack, modern enough to deter all enemies and nimble enough to defend our vital interests. We also need a foreign policy that protects American interests and encourages stability and not chaos.

At home conservatives understand that government is the problem, not the solution. Conservatives should not circum to a government inept at home who somehow succeeds in building nations abroad. I envision a national defense unparalleled, undefeatable and unencumbered by overseas nation building. I envision a national defense that promotes peace as President Reagan put it, peace through strength.

I believe in applying Reagan's approach of foreign policy to the Iran issue. Successful negotiations with untrustworthy adversaries is only achieved through a position of strength.

We brought Iran to the table through sanctions that I voted for. Now we must stay strong, that's why I cosponsored legislation that ensures that any deal between the U.S. and Iran, must be approved by congress. **Not only is that good policy it's the law.** It concerns me that the Iranians have a different interpretation of the agreement. They are putting out statements completely opposite of what we are saying. It concerns me that we may attempt, or the president may attempt to unilaterally and prematurely hold sanctions.

I will oppose any deal that does not end Iran's nuclear ambitions and have strong verification measures. I will insist that the final decision be brought before congress. The difference between President Obama and me, he seems to think he can negotiate from a position of weakness. Yet everyone needs to know that negotiations are not inherently bad. The trust but verify is required in any negotiation, but that our goal is or should always be peace, not war. We must realize though we do not project strength by borrowing money from China to send it to Pakistan.

Let's quit building bridges in foreign countries and use that money to build bridges here at home. It angers me to see moms burning our flag and shouting death to America in foreign countries that receive millions of dollars in foreign aid. I say it must end I say not one penny more to these haters of America.

To defend our country we do need to gather intelligence on the enemy, but when the intelligence Director is not punished for lying under oath, how are we suppose to trust our government agencies?

Warrantless searches of Americans phones and computers are un American and a threat to our civil liberties. I say your phone records are yours. I say the phone records are none of their damn business. The president created this vast dragnet by executive order and as president on day one **I will immediately end this unconstitutional surveillance.** I believe we can have liberty and security. I will not compromise your liberty for a false set of security, not now, not ever. We must defend ourselves but we must never give up who we are as a people. We must never diminish the Bill of rights as we fight this long war against evil.

We must believe in our founding documents we must protect economic and personal liberty again. America has much greatness left in her. We will thrive when we believe in ourselves again. I see an America strong enough to deter foreign aggression, yet wise enough to avoid unnecessary intervention. I see an America where criminal justice is applied equally and any law that disproportionately incarcerates people for color is repealed. I see an America with a restrained IRS that cannot target cannot harass American citizens for their political or religious beliefs. I see our big cities once again shinning and beaconing with creativity and ingenuity with American companies offering American jobs.

Let the debates begin and see who is real and who is lost.

Trump is Real, he tells it like it is. He is not a politician he is an American. It is he who has started the drive on illegal immigration. Rand Paul's speech was good, he hit on a lot of key areas, but it is his speech and it had been prepared ahead of time. We have to look at each candidate in that manner, even Donald Trump. Americans want someone who is action, not just talk. Let's look at one more candidate before we head back to more issues of importance.

Senator Marco Rubio Campaign speech

"After months of deliberation and prayer about the future of our country I come here tonight to make an announcement on how I believe I can best serve you. I chose to make this announcement at the freedom tour because it is truly a symbol of our country as a land of opportunity.

I am more confident than ever that despite our troubles we have it within our power to make our time another America century. In this very room five decades ago tens of thousands of exiles began their new lives in America. Their story is part of the larger story of the miracle of America. How united by common faith and their God given right to go as far as their talent and work would take them. A collection of immigrants and exiles, of former slaves and refuges together built the freest and most prosperous nation ever.

See for almost all of human history power and wealth belonged to only a select few. Most people who have ever lived were trapped by their circumstances of their birth; destine to live the lives their parents had. Americas different cause, here we are the children and the grandchildren who refuse to accept this.

Both of my parents were born to poor families in Cuba. After his mother died, my father had to go work when he was nine years old.

My mother was one of seven girls raised by a disabled father who struggled to provide for his family.

When they were young my parents had big dreams for themselves, but because they were not born in to wealth or power. Their future was destined to be defined by their past, so in 1956 they came here to America. The one place on earth where the aspirations of people like them could be more than just dreams.

Here in America my father became a bartender, my mother a cashier, a maid, a K-Mart stock clerk. They never made it big, but they were successful two immigrants with little education. They found stable jobs, owned a home. Retired with security and gave all four of their children a better life than their own.

My parents achieved what has become known as the American dream. The problem is now to many Americans are doubting whether that dream is still possible. Hard working families that are living paycheck to paycheck that are one expected expense away from disaster. Young Americans unable to start a career, business or family, because they owe thousands of dollars in student loans for degrees that did not even lead to jobs and small business owners who are left to struggle under the weight of more taxes, more regulations and more government.

Why is this happening in a country in more than two centuries that has been defined by a quality of opportunity? It's because while our people and our economy are pushing the boundaries of the twenty first century, too many of our leaders and ideas are stuck in the twentieth century.

They're busy looking backwards, so they do not see how the jobs and prosperity today depend to compete in a global economy and so our leaders put us at a disadvantage, by taxing, borrowing and regulating like it was 1999.

They look for solutions of yesterday so they do not see the good paying modern jobs require different skills and more education than in the past, so they blindly support a higher education outdated system that is too expensive, too inaccessible to those who need it most and they have forgotten, they have forgotten when America fails to lead global chaos inevitably follows.

They appease our enemies; they betray our allies and they weaken our military. Now look, the turn of the nineteenth century. A generation of Americans harnessed the power of the industrial age and they transformed this country into the leading economy in the world and the twentieth century became the American century. Well now the time has come for our generation to lead the way to a new American century.

If we reform our tax code and reduce regulations and control spending and modernize our immigration laws and appeal or replace Obama care. If we do these things Americans will create millions of better paying jobs. If we create a twentieth century higher education that provides American people a chance to acquire the necessary skills they need, that we no longer graduate students with mountains of debt, degrees that do not lead to jobs.

Graduate more high school students from high school ready to work, then our people will be ready to seize their opportunities in this economy.

If we remember the family, not the government is the most important institution in our society, if we remember all humane life deserves protection from the law. If we remember that all parents deserve to chose the education that's right for their children's education, then we will have a strong people and a nation and if America again should accept the mantle of global leadership.

By abandoning this administration's dangerous concessions to Iran and its hostility to Israel By reversing the hollowing out of our military, by giving our men and women in uniform resources and care the gratitude that they deserve, by no longer being passive in the face of the Chinese and Russian aggression and by ending the near total disregard for the erosion and democracy and human rights around the world especially Cuba, Venezuela and Nicaragua.

Then, if we did these things then our nation would be safer, our world more stable, our people more prosperous. These are the things we must do, but this election is not just about what laws we are going to pass. This election is about a generational choice, what kind of country we will be.

Now just yesterday a leader from yesterday began a campaign for president by promising to take us back to yesterday.

Yesterday is over, and we are never going back. You see we Americans are proud of our history, but our country has always been about the future and before us now is the opportunity to author the greatest chapter yet in the greatest story of America, but we can't do that by going back to the leaders and ideas of the past. We must change the decisions we are making by changing the people who are making them.

That is why tonight grounded by the lessons of our history, but inspired by the promise of our future I announce my candidacy for president of the United States I know my candidacy might seem improbable from abroad, after all in many countries the highest office in the land is reserved for the rich and the powerful, but I live in an exceptional country.

I live in an exceptional country where even the son of a bartender and a maid can have the same dreams. I live in an exceptional country where even the son of a bartender and a maid can have the same dream as those that come from power and privilege. I recognize the challenges of this campaign and I recognize the demands of this office that I seek. When this endeavor of all things I find comfort in the ancient command. Be strong and courageous. Do not tremble or be dismayed for the Lord your God is with you where ever you go.

I've heard some suggest that I should step aside and wait my turn. But I cannot. Because I believe our very identity an exceptional nation is at stake and I can make a difference as president.

I'm humbled by the realization by America, America doesn't owe me anything.

I have a debt to America that I must try and repay. This isn't just a country where I was born. America is literally the place that has changed my family's history.

I regret that my father didn't get to see this day in person. He used to tell me all the time, he used to tell us all the time, in this country you can achieve all the things you never could. In the days I'm tired or discouraged. I remember the sound of his keys jingling at the front door of our home well past midnight as he returned from another long day at work. When I was younger I didn't appreciate all he did for us, but now as my own children grow older, I more fully understand it. See my father was grateful for the work he had, but that was not the life he wanted for his children. He wanted all the dreams he had for himself to come true for us.

He wanted all the doors that closed for him to open for me, so my father stood behind a small portable bar in the back of a room for all those years, so tonight I can stand behind this podium in front of this room and this nation That journey from behind that bar, behind this podium that's the essence of the American dream. Whether we remain a special country will depend on whether that journey is still possible for those trying to make it right now.

The single mother that works long hours for little pay so her children don't have to struggle the way she had to, the young student who takes two busses before dawn, to attend a better school across town.

The workers in our hotel kitchens, the landscaping crews in our neighborhoods, the late night janitorial that clean our offices and even the bartenders that are standing in the back room in a bar somewhere in America, if their dreams in America become impossible we'll just have become another country, but if they succeed this twenty first century will also be an American century.

This will be the message of my campaign and the purpose of the presidency. To succeed on this journey I will need your prayers and your support and ultimately your vote. So tonight I am asking you take that first step by joining us at our web site **Marco Rubio.com** My wife Jeannette and four children are here tonight.

The next nineteen months will take me far away from home. I will miss watching Amanda run track and Daniel play volleyball and Anthony play football and Dominique play soccer. I have chosen this course because this election is about them; theirs is the most important generation in America. I will tell you why, because if we can capture the promise of this new century they will be the freest and most prosperous Americans who ever lived. If we fail they will be the first generation of Americans to inherit a country that is worse off than the country that was left to their parents. The final verdict of Americans will be written by Americans who have not yet been born. Let us make sure they record we made the right choice. That in the early years of this century faced with a rapidly changing and uncertain world, our generation rose to face the challenges of our time and because we did there was still one place in the world where who you come from does not determine how far you go.

Because we did, the American miracle lived on
Because we did, our children and their children lived in a
new American century Thank you.

Marco Rubio too had a great speech, and I think he is real
and sincere as well, but I think there are those that may
try to bully him and whether or not he has the stamina to
take on the hostile politicians with other hidden agendas
is unknown. But I do like his speech as well.

Remember I am writing this trying to be fair and a part of
me will be pushing for certain candidates more than
others, but if you know this in advance you will at least be
able to judge me on being honest and will agree or
disagree on those facts.

CHAPTER THREE

We are now going to look at the **Bill of Rights**. And see how they fit into America's History. This is another area that the presidential candidates will have to address at some point in their run for President.

Amendment 1

Congress shall make no law respecting an establishment of religion, or prohibiting the free exercise thereof; or abridging the freedom of speech, or of the press; or the right of the people peaceably to assemble, and to petition the government for a redress of grievances.

We all have a right to our religious beliefs, but when our government makes it legal for same sex marriages in some States are they not impeding on Church and States? In the military the same government uses the don't ask don't tell policy. President Obama is big about scolding the Christian while he looks away from the Muslim extremist who seek only to kill.

Let's look at President Obama who has done nothing but feed hatred on racial tensions and enable through sending the wrong message, that it is understandable that violence is needed to get your word out. Let's not forget the words to peaceably assemble under the 1st Amendment. The Democratic party only seems to pacify the racially divided groups, focusing on their own agendas, which is care taking the poor and uneducated only for the purpose of more control later.

This makes me think of home schooling rather than public schooling, not letting the kids deal with reality and consequences through peers of their own, but rather through the government that acts as the parent with total control.

Amendment 2

A well regulated militia, being necessary to the security of a free state, the right of the people to keep and bear arms, shall not be infringed.

Here we will see who is for gun control and who is against it. We have the right to keep and bear arms it says that right above here in the 2nd Amendment. Sure some have lost that right by committing crimes with guns or other stipulations, such as being an illegal alien. Once again Donald Trump has stated he is against the behaviors of those that commit crimes not the guns themselves. I am on his side there. It is obvious to those that think logically, criminals always find ways to steal, rob, rape, and even kill.

If we just take a few minutes and look at some statistics that are on the FBI's own Home page you will understand the need and the right of the 2nd Amendment.

The following information is covering a 5 year span between 2009 and 2013.

There were 73,834 murders.

108,612 rapes were recorded there were 1,832,659 robberies 790,172 were located on streets and highways.

243,842 were committed in commercial houses.

43,981 robberies took place at gas stations.

94,652 were located in a convenience stores

310,538 were in the residences. Do you think there should be concern on the American people's right to keep and bear arms?

Amendment 3

No soldier shall, in time of peace be quartered in any house, without the consent of the owner, nor in time of war, but in a manner to be prescribed by law.

Amendment 4

The right of the people to be secure in their persons, houses, papers, and effects, against unreasonable searches and seizures, shall not be violated, and no warrants shall issue, but upon probable cause, supported by oath or affirmation, and particularly describing the place to be searched, and the persons or things to be seized.

Rand Paul does speak of this in his presidential speech. Obama on the other hand seems to ignore our constitutional rights as the White House uses Homeland Security to justify where convenient. Hillary Clinton can't be trusted so anything with her is bound to end up a scandal.

Amendment 5

No person shall be held to answer for a capital, or otherwise infamous crime, unless on a presentment or indictment of a grand jury, except in cases arising in the land or naval forces, or in the militia, when in actual service in time of war or public danger; nor shall any person be subject for the same offense to be twice put in jeopardy of life or limb; nor shall be compelled in any criminal case to be a witness against himself, nor be deprived of life, liberty, or property, without due process of law; nor shall private property be taken for public use, without just compensation.

Amendment 6

In all criminal prosecutions, the accused shall enjoy the right to a speedy and public trial, by an impartial jury of the state and district wherein the crime shall have been committed, which district shall have been previously ascertained by law, and to be informed of the nature and cause of the accusation; to be confronted with the witnesses against him; to have compulsory process for obtaining witnesses in his favor, and to have the assistance of counsel for his defense.

If we look at this Amendment, we will see that President Obama has been consistent with ensuring fair trials are swayed, kicking the word impartial to the curb as he did in the Michael Brown ordeal in Ferguson, Missouri, Trayvon Martin in Florida, And the officers in Baltimore in the death of Freddie Gray.

When our own President of the United States directs havoc and sits back only to observe the aftermath, you have to ask what other ruinations does he have in store for us?

Amendment 7

In suits at common law, where the value in controversy shall exceed twenty dollars, the right of trial by jury shall be preserved, and no fact tried by a jury, shall be otherwise reexamined in any court of the United States, than according to the rules of the common law.

Amendment 8

Excessive bail shall not be required, nor excessive fines imposed, nor cruel and unusual punishments inflicted.

Again when we look at the riots both in Ferguson as well as Baltimore were not the citizens of the community punished by their government leaders who sat idly by and enabled those adults with juvenile behaviors to rob, loot, and destroy citizens in their own communities?

I blame the President of the United States on this by his carefully orchestrated words as he drifted in and out of the media to stir chaos.

Amendment 9

The enumeration in the Constitution, of certain rights, shall not be construed to deny or disparage others retained by the people.

Amendment 10

The powers not delegated to the United States by the Constitution, nor prohibited by it to the states, are reserved to the states respectively, or to the people.

I am no lawyer, these are just my opinions added in, as I ask questions of our Bill of Rights. As we look ahead at these presidential candidates, should we not look back at the current President and learn from his mistakes, and weaknesses. Should we not want to improve rather than ignore?

When looking for our next president should we hope for someone who is honest, trustworthy, smart, and ready, willing to fight for us? I would like that. I want Americans to be proud to be Americans.

Let's look at a few more presidential candidates and see what they have to say. Remember this is our country we are looking for the best candidate that will serve us, not us serve them.

<u>Ted Cruz Presidential speech</u>

He spoke at the largest Christian university in the world, Liberty University as he started off with "God bless Liberty University." Ted Cruz's mom was the first person in their family to go to college. In 1956 she graduated from Rice University with a degree in math and became a pioneering computer programmer in the 1950's and 1960's.

"Imagine a teenage boy not much older than you guys today, growing up in Cuba jet black hair skinny as a rail. Involved in student council and yet Cuba was not at a peaceful time. The dictator Batista was corrupt, he was oppressive and this teenage boy joins a revolution. He joins a revolution against Batista; he begins fighting with other teenagers, to free Cuba from the dictator.

This boy at age seventeen finds himself thrown in prison, finds himself tortured beaten and then at age eighteen he flees Cuba. He comes to America. Imagine for a second the hope that was in his heart as he rode that ferry boat across the Key West and got on a greyhound bus to head to Austin, Texas. To begin washing dishes making fifty cents an hour. Coming to the one land on earth, that has welcomed so many millions. When my dad came to America in 1957 he could not have imagined what lay in store for him.

Imagine a young married couple living together in the 1970's neither one of them has a personal relationship with Jesus. They have a little boy and they're both drinking far too much. They're living a fast life.

When I was three my father decided to leave my mother and me. We were living in Calvary at the time he got on a plane and flew back to Texas. He decided he didn't want to be married anymore, that he didn't want to be a father to his three year old son. Yet when he was in Houston a friend and colleague invited him to a bible study, invited him to Clairol Baptist church. There my father gave his life to Jesus Christ. God transformed his heart, so he drove to the airport, he bought a plane ticket and he flew back to be with my mother and me.

There are people who wonder if faith is real? I can tell you in my family there is not a second of doubt, because were it not for the transformative love I would not have been saved and would have been raised by a single mom and not my father in the house. Imagine another little girl living in Africa in Kenya and Nigeria, a diverse crowd. (Everyone laughing)

Playing with kids they spoke Swahili she spoke English. Coming back to California, after her parents who had been missionaries in Africa raised her on the central coast. She starts a small business when she's in grade school baking bread she calls it Heidi's Bakery. She and her brother compete baking bread they bake thousands of loafs of bread and go to a local apple orchard where they sale the bread to people coming to pick apples.

She goes on to a career in business, excelling and rising to the highest pinnacles and then Heidi becomes my wife and my very best friend in the world. Heidi becomes an incredible mom to our two precious little girls Caroline and Katharine, the joys and loves of our life.

Imagine another teenage boy being raised in Houston hearing stories from his dad about prison and torture in Cuba. Hearing stories about how fragile liberty is beginning to study the United States Constitution. Learning about the incredible protections we have in this country that protects the liberty of every God living American in this country.

Experiencing the challenges at home in the mid 1980's oil prices cratered and his parents business go bankrupt. Heading off to school over a thousand miles from home in a place he knew nobody. Where he was alone and scared and his parents going through bankruptcy meant there was no financial support at home.

So at the age of seventeen he went to get two jobs to help pay his way through school. He took over a hundred thousand dollars in school loans. Well a lot of you I suspect can relate too. Loans I'll point out I paid off just a few years ago.

These are all of our stories, these are who we are as Americans and yet the promise of America seems more and more distant. What is the promise of America? The idea, the revolutionary idea that this country was founded upon is that our rights they don't come from man, they come from God almighty and the purpose of the constitution as Thomas Jefferson put it is to serve as chains to bind the mischief of government.

The incredible opportunity of the American dream is that it has enabled millions of people, from all over the world to come to America with nothing and to achieve anything.

Then the American exceptionalism, which has made this nation a clarion voice for freedom in the world a shining city on the hill. That is the promise to America.

That's what makes this nation an indispensable nation, a unique nation in the history of the world. Yet so many today find that promise un-detainable. So many fear it is slipping away from our hands.

I want to talk to you this morning about reuniting the promise of America two hundred and forty years ago on this very day a thirty eight year old lawyer named Patrick Henry stood up just a hundred miles from here in Richmond Virginia and said **give me liberty, or give me death.**

I want to ask each of you to imagine, imagine millions of conservative Americans all across America rising up together to say in unison **we demand our liberty.** Today roughly half born again Christians aren't voting. They are staying home. Imagine instead millions of people of faith coming from all across America. Coming out to the polls and voting our values. Today millions of young people are scared worried about the future, worried what the future will hold. Imagine millions of young people coming together and saying, we will stand for liberty.

Think just how different the world would be. Imagine instead of economic stagnation, boom economic growth. Instead of small businesses going out of business in record numbers, imagine small businesses growing and prospering . Imagine young people coming out of school with four, five, or six job offers.

Imagine innovation driving on the internet as government regulators and tax collectors are kept at bay and more and more opportunity is created.

Imagine America finally becoming energy self sufficient as millions and millions of jobs are created. Five years ago today, the president signed Obama care into law. Within hours Liberty University went to court filing a lawsuit to stop that failed law.

Instead of the joblessness, instead of the millions forced into part time work, instead of the millions that have lost their health care insurance and lost their doctors of faith sky rocketing insurance healthcare premiums.

Imagine in 2017 a new president signing legislation appealing every word of Obama care. Imagine healthcare reform that keeps government out of the way between you and your doctor and makes healthcare insurance personable, portable and affordable.

Instead of a tax code that crushes innovation, that imposes burdens families struggling to make ends meet. Imagine a simple flat tax that lets every American fill out their taxes on a post card. Imagine abolishing the IRS instead of the lawlessness and the president's unconstitutional executive amnesty.
Imagine a president that finally, finally, finally secures the borders. Imagine a legal immigration system that welcomes and celebrates those that come to achieve the American dream.

Instead of a Federal government that wages an assault on our religious liberty, that goes after **Hobby Lobby** that goes after **little sisters of the poor** that goes after **Liberty University.** Imagine a federal government that stands for the first amendment rights of every American. Instead of a federal government that works to undermine our values.

Imagine a federal government that works to defend human sanctity of human life, to up hold the sacrament of marriage. Instead of a government that undermines our second amendment rights. That seeks to band our ammunition. Imagine a federal government that protects the rights to keep and bear arms of all law abiding Americans.

Instead of a government that seizes your emails and your cell phones. Imagine a government that protected the privacy right of every American.

Instead of federal government that seeks to dictate school curriculum through common core. Imagine repealing every word of common core.

Imagine embracing school choices as the civil rights issue of the next generation. That every single child regardless of race, regardless of ethnicity, regardless of wealth, or zip code every child in America has a right to a quality education.

That is true from all of the above whether public schools, or charter schools, or private schools, Christian schools, or parochial schools, or home schools every child.

Instead of a president who boycotts Prime minister Netanyahu. Imagine a president who stands unapologetic with Israel. Instead of a president that seeks to go to the United Nations to run congress and the American people. Imagine a president that says he will honor the constitution and under no circumstances will Iran be allowed to acquire a nuclear weapon.

Imagine a president who will stand up and say we will defeat radical Islamic terrorism and we will call it by its name. We will defend the United States of America. Now all of these seem difficult indeed to some they may seem unimaginable and yet if you look in the history of our country, imagine it's 1775 and you and I were sitting there in Richmond listening to Patrick Henry say **Give me liberty or give me death**. Imagine its 1776 and we were watching the fifty four signers of the Declaration of Independence stand together and pledge their lives, their fortunes and their sacred honor to igniting the promise to America.

Imagine it was 1777 and we were watching General Washington as he lost battle after battle after battle, in the freezing cold, soldiers with no shoes were dying fighting for freedom against the most powerful army in the world. That too seemed unimaginable.

Imagine in 1933 and we were listening to Franklin D. Roosevelt tells America at a crushing time of depression in a gathering storm abroad, that we have nothing to fear but fear itself, imagine it's 1979 and you and I were listening to Ronald Reagan and he was telling us that we would cut the top marginal tax rate from seventy percent all the way down to twenty eight percent.

That we would go from crushing stagnation to booming economic growth, to millions being lifted out of poverty into prosperity in abundance.

At the very day he was sworn in, our hostages who were relinquishing in Iran would be released. Within a decade we would win the cold war and tear the Berlin wall to the ground, that would have seemed unimaginable and yet with the grace of God that is exactly what happened.

From the dawn of this country at every stage America has enjoyed God's providential blessing, over and over again when we face impossible odds. The American people rose to the challenge. You know compared to that repealing the Obama care and abolishing the IRS isn't all that tough.

The power of the American people when we rise up and stand for liberty knows no bounds If you are ready to join a grass roots army across this nation coming together and standing for liberty.

I'm going to ask you to break a rule here today and take out your cell phones and text the word constitution to the number 33733, you can also text the word imagine to the same number its reversible.
Once again, text constitution 33733 God blessing his bid on America from the very beginning of this nation, I believe God isn't done with America yet. I believe in you I believe in the power of millions of courageous conservatives rising up to reignite the promise of America. That is why today I am announcing I am running for the president of the United States.

Dr. Ben Carson presidential announcement.

"I am Ben Carson and I am a candidate for the President of the United States. America remains a place for dreams. A lot of people are down on our nation. They want to point out all the bad things that have happened here. Have you ever noticed there are a lot of people trying to get in here and not a lot of them trying to escape?"

"It says something and it was a place of dreams for my mother. My mother came from a very large rural family from Tennessee and was shuffled from home to home She always had a desire for education, but she was never able to get beyond the third grade. She married at the age thirteen in hopes of escaping a desperate situation. She and my father moved here to Detroit he worked factory. In fact I remember one Christmas being right here in this auditorium sitting right over there for GM employees. They were having a Christmas program."

"Some years later my mother discovered he was a bigamist, he had another family and that occasion to divorce him, you know she only had a third grade education and consequently we were thrown in to a situation of dire poverty. She still maintained that dream of education, but now it's for us more so than for her.

"We moved in with her older sister and brother in-law in Boston, typical tenement large multi family dwelling, boarded up windows and doors, gangs, murders. Both of our older cousins who we adored were killed. I remember when our favorite drug dealer was killed, Vinnie Boston Borrows. He drove a blue Cadillac."

"You know they used to bring us candy, so we liked to see the drug dealers. You know they're rats, they're roaches. In the more upscale neighborhoods they called them water bugs, but we knew what they were. My mother was out working extraordinary hard. She sometimes did three jobs at a time. She was trying to stay off welfare and the reason for that was most the people she saw go on welfare never came off of it."

"She didn't want to be dependent on it and she wanted us to be independent. She decided she would work as long and as hard as necessary. Leaving at five in the morning and getting back after midnight day after day after day, doing what other people didn't want to do, trying to maintain her independence and she was very thrifty."

"She would drive the car till it wouldn't make the sound and then she would collect her nickels and dimes and quarters and by a new car. Then people would say how does that woman afford a new car?
But she knew how to manage money and I'm fond of saying if my mother was in charge of the Secretary of Treasure we would not be in the deficit situation."

"You know there are many people that are critical of me because you know Carson wants to get rid of all the safety nets and welfare programs, even though he must have benefitted from them. This is a blatant lie."

"I have no desire to get rid of safety nets for people who need them. I have a strong desire to get rid of programs that create dependency, in able body people.

"We are not doing people a favor when we tap them on the head and tell them there, there you poor little thing we are going to take care of all your needs. You don't have to worry about anything. You know who else said things like that? Socialist and their programs always end up looking the same. They want to take care of people from cradle to grave, but they want to be involved in every aspect of their lives and they want most of their earnings, but they say it will be a utopia and nobody will have to worry."

"The problem is all of those societies, end up looking the same, with a small group of elites at the top, controlling everything a rampantly diminishing middleclass and a vastly expanding dependent class."

"That was not the intention for this country. This country was envisioned by individuals who wanted everything to be around surrounding the people, of, for and by the people. Not of, for and by the government and the government was to respond to the will of the people, not the people to the will of the government."

" We have allowed the whole thing to be turned upside down and I am not an anti government person by any stretch of the imagination. I think the government as described in our constitution is wonderful, but now we have gone far beyond what our constitution describes.

We have just allowed it to expand based on what the political class wants. They like to increase their power and dominion over the people and I think it is time for the people to rise up and take their government back. Now the political class won't like me to say stuff like that."

"I'll tell you a secret political class comes from both parties. It comes from all over the place. It includes unfortunately even the media now. The press is the only business in America that is protected by our constitution. You have to ask yourself why they are the only ones protected."

"It is because our founders envisioned a press that was on the side of the people. Not a press that was on the side of the democrats or the Republicans, or the Federates or anti Federates.

This is a direct appeal to media, you guys have an almost sacred position in a true democracy please don't abuse it.

My mother's dream was to move back to Detroit and we were eventually able to do that, but I was a terrible student and my brother was a terrible student and she didn't know what to do, so she prayed she asked God for wisdom.

You know what you don't have to have a PHD to talk with God. You just have to have faith and God gave her the wisdom at least in her opinion, my brother and I didn't think it was that wise. Turning off the TV and reading submitting to written book reports when she couldn't read.

You know it didn't matter because it worked. As I started reading those books which I didn't really want to. I started reading about people and their accomplishments and I started realizing the person who has the most to do with your life is you not somebody else.

It is the can do attitude that made this country succeed. People worked together if a farmer got injured the others would harvest his crops to help him. If somebody got killed there were others to take care of their families. That's who we are we take care of Americans.

People are afraid to stand up for what they believe in they don't want to offend or be called a name they don't want an IRS audit. They don't want their jobs or families messed with. "There were a couple WWII veterans there and they were thanking me. I said no it is me who should be thanking you."

He talked about the brave men and women in our military thanking them. We have to start opening our mouths for the values and morale of America. He stated he does not want to be a politician he wants to do what is right for America.

He stated the Baltimore incident. That many think there is no hope. Many people are buying into our economy is getting much better. The unemployment rate was down to 5.5 percent. You know if our unemployment was down to that we would be humming. He stated stop being loyal to a party or a man that is the key to success in our country.

We need to make sure the next president is more interested in helping the next generation then the next election. Dr. Ben Carson had more to say on tax cuts. Check out his speech on you tube.

Rick Perry's Presidential speech

" Thank You very much. I love you Honey. You know I was born five years after a global war that killed more than 60 million people. I am a son of a veteran of that war who flew 35 missions over war torn Europe as a tail gunner on a B-17. When dad returned home, married mom and started a life together. They were raised during a time of great hardship, and had little expectation beyond living in peace, putting a roof over our heads, and putting food on our table. Home was a place called Paint Creek, Texas. Too small to be called a town, but it was the center of my universe.

For years we had an outhouse, mom bathed us on the back porch in a number two wash tub. She also hand sewed my clothes till I went off to college. I attended Paint Creek Rural school, grades one through twelve. Played six man football, was a member of the Boy Scouts troop 48, became an eagle scout.

I went off to Texas A&M where I was a member of the Corp Cadet. I got my degree in animal science. I was proud to wear the uniform of an Air Force officer as an Aircraft Commander. After serving I returned home. I returned home to those rolling plains, and that big oh sky of West Texas and returned to farming. There is no person on earth more optimistic than a dry land cotton farmer. We all know there is a good rain just around the corner, no matter how long you been waiting. The values learned on my families cotton farm are timeless.

The dignity of your work, the integrity of your word, responsibility to community, the unbreakable bonds of family, and duty to country. These are enduring values. Not some product of some idyllic past, but a touchstone of American life in our small towns, in our largest cities, and in our booming suburbs. I've seen America life, I've seen it from the red dirt of a West Texas cotton field, from a campus in College Station, Texas, from an elevated view of a C-130 cockpit, and from the office of the Governor of Texas.

I had the great privilege to serve a rural community in the Texas Legislature, and I lead the 12th largest economy. I know that America has experienced great change, but what it means to be an American has never changed.

We are the only nation in the world founded on the power of an idea that all, that all are created equal, that they are endowed by their creator with certain un alien rights, and among these are life and liberty, and the pursuit of happiness.

Our rights come from God not from government. Our people are not subjects of government, but instead government is subject to the people. It has always been the case that this social compact between one generation and the next, to pass along an inheritance of a stronger country full of greater promise and possibility, and that's social compact and it has been protected at great sacrifice. It was never more clear to me then when I took my father to the American cemetery that overlooks the bluffs at Omaha Beach.

On that peaceful windswept setting, there lay 9,000 braves, including 45 pairs of brothers, 33 of whom are buried side by side. A father and a son, 2 sons of a president. They all traded their future for ours in a final act of loving sacrifice.

In that American cemetery it is no accident that each headstone faces West, West over the Atlantic toward the nation they defended the nation they love, the nation they would never come home to. It struck me as I stood in the midst of those heroes, that they look upon us in silent judgment, and that we must ask ourselves, are we worthy of their sacrifice?

The truth is we are at the end of an era of failed leadership. We have been lead by a divider who has sliced and diced the electric, pinning American against American for political purposes. 6 years into this so called recovery, and I might add our economy is barely growing. This winter it actually got smaller. Our economic slowdown is not inevitable, it just happens to be the result of bad economic policy.

The president's tax and regulatory policies have slammed the door shut of opportunity on the average American who is trying to climb the economic ladder. Resigning the middle class to stagnant wages, to personal debt to defer dreams.

Weakness at home has lead to weakness abroad. The world has descended into chaos of this presidents own making.

While his White House Loyalist construct an alternative universe, where Isis is contained, the remedy is merrily a setback. Where the nature of the enemy can't be acknowledge for fear of offense. Where the world's largest sponsor of terrorism, the Islamic Republic of Iran can be trusted to live up to a nuclear agreement.

No decision has done more harm than the president's decision to withdraw our troops from Iraq. Let no one be mistaken, leaders of both parties have made grave, grave mistakes, but in January of 2009, when Barack Obama became Commander and Chief, Iraq had been largely pacified.
America had won the war, but our president had failed to secure the peace. How callus it seems now. Cities once secured with American blood, are now being taken by Americas enemies, all because of a campaign slogan. I saw during Vietnam a war where politicians didn't keep faith with the sacrifices and courage of America's fighting men and women. Where men were ordered into combat without the full support of their civilian Commanders.

To see it happen again 40 years later because of political gainsmanship and dishonesty is a national disgrace. My friends we are a resilient country You think about who we are, we've been through a Civil war we've been through 2 world wars, we made it through the great depression, we even made it through Jimmy Carter. We will make it through the Obama years, we will do this.

You know the fundamental nature of our country is our people never stay knocked down. We get back up, we dust ourselves off, we move forward, and you know what, we will do it again.

I want to share some important truths with my fellow Americans today, starting with this truth. We don't have to settle for a world of chaos and an America that shrinks from its responsibilities, we don't have to apologize for American exceptionalism, or Western values. We don't have to accept slow growth that leaves behind the middle class, that leaves millions of Americans out of work, we don't have to settle for crumbling bureaucracies that target tax payers and harm our veterans. We don't have to resign ourselves to death, decay, slow growth.

We have the power to make things new again, to project America's strength again, and get our economy going again. And that is why today I am running for the presidency of the United States of America.

It's time to create real jobs, to increase wages, to create opportunity for all. To give every citizen a stake in this country. To restore hope, real hope to forgotten Americans. You know there are millions of middleclass families who have just given up hope of getting ahead, millions of workers out there that have given up hope of just finding a job, and yea it's time for a reset. Time to reset the relationship between government and citizen.

Think of the arrogance in Washington D.C. representing itself as some big and wisdom, with policies that are smothering this vast land, with no regard to what makes each State and community unique, that's just wrong. We need to return power to the States and freedom to the individual. Today our citizens and entrepreneurs are burden by over regulation and unspeakable debt and that's not just physical nightmare, it's a moral failure.

I want to speak to the millennial people just a moment. This massive debt is passed on from our generation to yours. This is breaking of a social compact and you deserve better. I'm going to offer a better plan to fix the entitlement system and to stop this theft from your generation.

To those Americans, to those I might add forgotten Americans drowning in debt, working harder for wages that don't keep up with the rising cost of living. I came here today to say I hear you.
 I know you face rising health care costs, rising child care costs, sky rocketing tuition costs, mounting student loan debt, I hear you and I am going to do something about it.

To the one in five children that's families are on food stamps, to the one in seven Americans living in poverty, to the one in ten workers who are under employed, unemployed, are just tired and given up I hear you, you are not forgotten.

I am running to be your president. To those small businesses on main street that are just struggling to get by, that are smothered by regulation. They're targeted by Dodd Frank. I hear you, you are not forgotten. Your time is coming. The American people they see this red game, the insiders get rich the middleclass pay the tab. There is something wrong when the Dow is near record high and small businesses on main street can't even get a loan. Since when did capitalism involve the elimination of risk where the biggest banks who are on regulation strangle our community banks? Capitalism is not corporatism. It is not a guarantee of reward without risk. It is not about Wall Street at the expense of Main Street.

The reason I am running for president is because I know that our country's best days lay ahead. There is nothing wrong in America today that a change of leadership will not make happen.

We're just a few good decisions away from unleashing economic growth and reviving the American dream. We need to fix a tax code that's riddled with loopholes that sends jobs overseas, that punishes success.

We got the highest corporate tax rate in the Western world, it's time to reduce it bring home jobs. Lift wages for those working families.

Do you realize by the time this administration gets done with its experiment with big government they will have added almost 600,000 pages of new regulation to the national register. On my first day in office I will issue an immediate freeze on pending regulations from the Obama administration. That same day I will send to Congress a comprehensive reform and rollback of job killing mandates created by Obama care, Dodd Frank, and other Obama era politicians.

Agencies will have to live under strict regulatory budgets, health insurers will have to earn the right to your money instead of lobbying Washington trying to force you to hand it over. On day one I will also sign an executive order approving the construction of the Keystone Pipeline.

Energy is vital to our economy and might I add to our national security. On day one I will sign an executive order authorizing the export of natural gas and all free European allies from the dependence of Russia's energy supplies.

Vladimir Putin uses oil to hold our allies hostage. So here's our message. If energy is going to be used as a weapon, America will have the largest arsenal. We will unleash an era of economic growth and limitless opportunity, we will rebuild America industry, we will lift wages for American workers.

It can be done, because it has been done, in Texas. During my 14 years as governor, Texas created almost one third of all new American jobs. In the last 7 years of my tenure Texas created 1.5 million new jobs, as a matter of fact without Texas America would have lost 400,000 jobs. We were the engine of growth, because we had a simple formula, you control spending and taxes, you implement smart regulations, you invest in an educated workforce, and you stop frivolous lawsuits.

Texas now has the second highest high school graduation rate in the country, and it has the highest graduation rate for African American and Hispanic students. We lead the nation in exports, including high tech exports. We passed historic tax relief, and I'm proud to have signed balanced budgets for fourteen years.

We not only created opportunity we stood for law and order, when there was a crisis at our border last year, and the president refused my invitation to see that challenge that we faced. I said Mr. President if you do not secure this border Texas will.

Because of that threat, because of that threat by those drug cartels and transnational gangs, I deployed the Texas National Guard. The policies worked, apprehensions declined by seventy percent. If you elect me your president I will secure that border.

Homeland security begins with border security. The most basic compact between a president and the people, is to keep the country safe. The great lesson of history is that strength and resolve bring peace, and order and weakness and vaccination create chaos, and conflict.

My very first act as president will be to resend any agreement with Iran that will legitimize their quest to get a nuclear weapon. Now is the time, now is the time for clear headed proven leadership. We have seen what happens when we elect a president based on media acclaim, rather than a record of accomplishment.

This will be a show me don't tell me election, where voters look past the rhetoric to the real record. The question of every candidate will be this, when have you lead? Leadership is not a speech on the Senate floor, it is not what you say, it is what you have done.

We will not find the kind of leadership needed to revitalize the country by looking to the political class in Washington. I've been tested I have lead the most successful State in America. I have dealt with crisis after crisis, from the disintegration of the space shuttle to Hurricanes Katrina, Ike, to the crisis at the border, and the first diagnosis in America.

I have brought together first responders, charities, and people of faith to house and heal citizens dealing with vulnerable tragedy. The spirit of compassion demonstrated by Texans is alive all across America today.

While we have experienced a deficit in leadership, among the American people there is a surplus of spirit. Among our people there is a spirit of selflessness, that we live to make the world better for our children, not just ourselves.

It was said that when King George the third asked what General George Washington would do in winning the war. He was told he would return to his farm and relinquish power, and to that the Monarch replied. If he does that he will be the greatest man of his age. George Washington lived in the service of a cause greater than self.

You know if anyone is still wondering if America still possess the character of selfless heroes? I'm here to say yes, I am surrounded by heroes. They're in all generations, they're in all the different generations, but they're all woven together by the same selfless sacrifice.

There are heroes like medal of honor Mike Thornton, who survived enemy ambush in Vietnam. Made it back to the safety of a water rescue, only to find out his fellow team member had been left behind presumed dead, but Mike didn't leave he returned through enemy fire, he retrieved Lieutenant Norris, who was still alive and then he swam for two hours keeping his wounded team mate afloat until they were rescued.

Heroes like Marcus Luttrell, he survived a savage attack on the side of a mountain in Afghanistan losing three of his team mates. I might add 16 warriors were shot down trying to rescue him. He is not just a lone survivor to Anita and me, he is a second son. Taya Kyle , Taya Kyle who suffered the deep loss of her husband Chris, an American hero. When I think of Taya Kyle, I think of a brave woman who not just carries the lofty burden of Chris's legacy, but the grief of every family who has lost a love one from this war or its difficult aftermath.

Anita and I want to thank Taya for her tremendous courage. America is an extraordinary country. Our greatness lies not in our government, but in our people. Each day Americans demonstrate tremendous courage, but many of those Americans have been knocked down. They're looking for a second chance, let's give them that second chance, let's give them real leadership, let's give them a future greater than the greatest days of our past.

Let's give them a president that leads them in the direction of our highest dreams, our best dreams, our highest hopes, and our greatest promise. Thank you and God bless you.

In order to call this home, one must except the responsibilities of this household.

Our current President has failed us, but America will rise to the occasion and elect a true American to lead us, not a Republican or Democrat, an American.

CHAPTER FOUR

This next chapter we are going to look at politics in action, as we look at Illinois specifically, so as to get a better understanding of political terminology. The presidential candidates are all running for the highest political office in the country, **The President of the United States**.

If we look at Illinois we will get a good idea of why so many Americans are fed up with our typical politicians. This is important to know because as we look at the presidential candidates They are all fighting not just for our vote but as the candidate for a particular party, that being Republican Party and Democratic Party.

Let's look at this Executive order by Governor Rauner and ask the questions that have yet to be answered. The people of Illinois deserve the best representation from their governor. The governor is elected to represent the people not take advantage of them. The following data came off the Official website of the Governor of Illinois.

EXECUTIVE ORDER 15-08

EXECUTIVE ORDER TO ADDRESS THE STATE'S FISCAL CRISIS

WHEREAS, the State of Illinois faces historic, unprecedented debt obligations, including over $100 billion in unfunded pension liabilities and $6.5 billion in unpaid bills; and

WHEREAS, although the Illinois Constitution requires – and the people of Illinois expect – a balanced and honest budget, the State's budget for the current fiscal year ending June 30, 2015, does not fully account for all expected spending or changes in revenue during the remainder of this fiscal year, resulting in a current deficit of approximately $760 million; and

WHEREAS, the budget for the current fiscal year relies upon borrowing, including $650 million in inter-fund borrowing; and

WHEREAS, the State is required to pay $1.4 billion per year to service debt on bonds previously issued to fund the State's pension obligations; and

WHEREAS, on top of the payments for pension-related debt, the State is expected to contribute $6.6 billion from the General Revenue Fund to the pension systems in the next fiscal year – which includes $4.6 billion in payments resulting from the State's previous failure to adequately funds its pension obligations; and

WHEREAS, the State's credit rating is currently the lowest among all 50 U.S. states; and

WHEREAS, the State's debts diminish the State's ability to attract and retain businesses and residents and are a burden upon the State's ability to serve the critical needs of its people; and

WHEREAS, in order to honestly align spending and revenues, to satisfy the requirements of Section 2 of Article VIII of the Illinois Constitution, and to ensure that our public resources are available for our most critical needs, the Executive Branch must undertake meaningful steps to examine and reduce spending;

THEREFORE, I, Bruce Rauner, Governor of Illinois, by virtue of the executive authority vested in me by Section 8 of Article V of the Constitution of the State of Illinois, do hereby order as follows:

I.   DEFINITIONS

As used in this Executive Order:

"CMS" means the Illinois Department of Central Management Services.

"FY 2015" means the fiscal year of the State of Illinois ending on June 30, 2015.

"GOMB" means the Governor's Office of Management and Budget.

"State Agency" means any officer, department, agency, board, commission, or authority of the Executive Branch of the State of Illinois.

"State Funds" means all funds available to a State Agency from whatever source.

II.   PROCUREMENT AND PERSONNEL

1.   Review of Procurement and Personnel Decisions. As soon as practicable, every State Agency shall provide a report to GOMB identifying (a) every contract or grant that was let, awarded, or entered into by the State Agency on or after November 1, 2014 and through the date of the report and (b) every decision or action taken by the

State Agency to employ or to terminate the employment of any employee of the State Agency on or after November 1, 2014 and through the date of the report.

2.   Contracts and Grants. Until July 1, 2015, no State Agency shall let, award, or enter into any contract or grant, or any amendment or change order to or renewal of any existing contract or grant, that obligates the expenditure of State Funds except as follows:

(a)   Contracts Required by Law. A State Agency may enter into a contract or grant that is required to comply with applicable law, provided that the State Agency first complies with any applicable guidelines issued by GOMB for verifying that the contract or grant is required by law.

(b)   Contracts for Emergency Expenditures. A State Agency may enter into a contract that is required in order to incur an emergency expenditure that, if not incurred, would jeopardize one or more fundamental operations of the State Agency and for which there is not adequate time to permit review and approval by GOMB before entering into the contract for, provided that (i) the contract does not obligate the expenditure of State Funds except as required for the emergency expenditure, and (ii) the State Agency complies with any applicable guidelines issued by GOMB for subsequent review of the contract and expenditure, including of the exigent circumstances that existed.

(c)   Contracts for Small Purchases. A State Agency may enter into a contract that obligates the State to pay less than $50,000 (including any contingent and conditional payment obligations) during the term of the contract,

Provided that the State Agency complies with any applicable guidelines issued by GOMB for subsequent review of the contract and expenditure.

(d) Contracts and Grants for Essential Operations. If the State Agency determines that the contract or grant is needed for its essential operations, but the contract does not otherwise meet the criteria immediately above, the State Agency must first submit the proposed contract or grant to GOMB for review and approval in accordance with any applicable guidelines issued by GOMB, before the State Agency enters into the contract or grant.

3. Review of the major Interstate Construction Projects. The planning and development of any major construction that has an impact on interstate travel and for which construction has not commenced as identified by the State Agency or GOMB, shall be suspended in order to allow careful review of the project and its potential costs and benefits.

4. Review and termination of Non-Essential Contracts. Every State Agency shall review all contracts that require the expenditure of State Funds that are not essential for the State Agency's operations. As soon as reasonably practicable, every State Agency shall provide a report to GOMB of all such non- essential contracts, together with information about when and under what circumstances such non- essential contracts may be terminated without material penalty to the State of Illinois.

III.   SPENDING

1. Managing Existing Resources. To the extent feasible and without compromising its essential operations, each State Agency shall take all necessary actions to manage its State Funds and other resources to avoid the need for supplemental funding in excess of the State Funds heretofore made available by appropriations or other sources. Each State Agency shall provide a report to GOMB as soon as practicable of such actions taken, or to be taken, by the State Agency.

2. Supplemental Funding (Balanced Budget Note Act). No State Agency shall encumber, obligate, or expend State Funds that have been appropriated pursuant to a "supplemental appropriation bill," as such term is defined in Section 5 of the Balanced Budget Note Act (25 ILCS 80/5), unless (1) such supplemental appropriation bill was accompanied by a Balanced Budget Note as required by the Balanced Budget Note Act or (2) otherwise approved by GOMB.

3. Motor Vehicles. No State Agency shall purchase or lease any motor vehicle except in accordance with any applicable guidelines issued by GOMB.

4. Out-of-State Travel. No State Agency shall expend State Funds for travel by its personnel, contractors, or other persons outside of the State of Illinois except after review and approval by GOMB.

5. In State Travel. Every State Agency shall make every effort to limit the number of its personnel who travel within the State of Illinois and seek reimbursement for the costs of such travel. Such efforts shall include:

(a) Pre- Approval for Reimbursements. Every employee must receive express pre- approval from the head of the agency in which the employee is employed, or the designee of such agency head, for any travel costs to be reimbursed by the State.

(b) Review of travel vouchers. Every State Agency must conduct a review of all travel vouchers that have been submitted and paid in order to identify and eliminate excessive, improper, un-approved, or unnecessary reimbursement.

(c) Eliminating Unnecessary Travel. To the extent feasible, every State Agency shall reduce reimbursements for travel costs by requirement employees to use State owned vehicles (where such usage results in a net savings to the State), to carpool, or take public transportation whenever possible: and by using teleconferencing and videoconferencing in place of travel whenever possible.

IV. STATE PROPERTY

1.Surplus Personal Property. At the direction of GOMB, CMS shall identify surplus personal property owned by the State of Illinois and conduct an auction of such property, in compliance with all applicable laws and regulations. CMS shall provide a report to GOMB of all such actions taken by June 30, 2015.

2. Surplus Real Property. GOMB and CMS shall review all real property owned or leased by the State of Illinois and develop and implement a comprehensive strategy for (1) consolidating offices and other functions into fewer and less costly spaces, (2) re-locating offices and other functions from leased space to space owned by the State of Illinois, and (3) disposing of under-utilized space.

3. Energy Efficiency and Conservation. Every State Agency shall implement practices to reduce energy consumption and prevent wasteful spending on energy, including reducing heating, air conditioning, and lighting usage when facilities are not in use. The facility manager for each State Agency shall recommend specific measures and practices that may be undertaken by the State Agency.

V.   PRIOR EXECUTIVE ORDERS

This Executive Order supersedes any contrary provision of any prior Executive Order.

VI.   SAVINGS CLAUSE

This Executive Order does not contravene and shall not be construed to contravene any State or federal law or any collective bargaining agreement.

VII.   SEVERABILITY CLAUSE

If any part of this Executive Order is found invalid by a court of competent jurisdiction, the remaining provisions shall remain in full force and effect.

VIII.   EFFECTIVE DATE

This Executive Order shall take effect immediately upon filing with the Secretary of State.

Bruce Rauner, Governor

Issued by Governor: January 12, 2015

Filed with Secretary of State: January 12, 2015

Why don't we ask why the pension is inadequately funded? The pension was set up to be self sustaining. So the only answer they can give you is that they misappropriated funds. This is political terminology for stealing, which is exactly what they have done. They try to play three ball Monty with other people's money as they the politicians, and those in high office always see to it they get paid first, and the rest of us have to suffer the consequence.

The budget is setup to fail when they say the budget for the current fiscal year relies upon borrowing, including $650 million in inter-fund borrowing; and

WHEREAS, the State is required to pay $1.4 billion per year to service debt on bonds previously issued to fund the State's pension obligations. If they had left the pension alone and not robbed from it, the State of Illinois would be in a much better situation.

If you or I had done this we would be in jail, yet the highest office in the State of Illinois run by our elected governor has continued to not only deny the problem, but refuses to fix the problem as he is only fixed on one agenda. He is wanting to destroy the unions.

They talk about identifying all the contracts that are out there, yet fail to honor the very contracts that they agreed to. The latest one I have heard about is the IOU's the State is offering to those that have won the State lottery. If they state they can't pay, and yet they are still receiving money from people who are unaware of this is this not criminal, if not unethical? This is fraud at the highest level.

As I just mentioned Governor Rauner is focused on destroying the unions, you might ask why? Could it be if the State of Illinois had no unions that business owners would be able to lower wages, reduce medical coverage and increase medical costs on your part further gapping the rich and the poor?

What about holding this office to the highest standard, while we honor our contracts with State employees. All you have to do is travel around the State and ask the gas stations if they take the State charge cards and if not why? You will see lots of places will tell you the State doesn't want to pay their bills. This can be seen with Doctors and medical institutions as State employees have to pay their cost up front sometimes the entire amount as the State employees wait to get reimbursed.

Unions are there to help represent the people who work hard for their money. Big corporations and Small businesses have lawyers working for them why shouldn't the rest of us Americans? This is an area the presidential candidates will have to address in their quest for the office of the presidency.

Illinois is just one State but if we could fix things one State at a time then America would be a greater more prosperous place to thrive. Let's continue on with a few more candidates as we try to wake America up to the seriousness of what is going on in our country.

It is interesting that the Constitution is good enough for the Governor as he states, I, Bruce Rauner, Governor of Illinois, by virtue of the executive authority vested in me by Section 8 of Article V of the Constitution of the State of Illinois, do hereby order as follows:

He states under State funding each State Agency should budget and manage their State Funds, yet they robbed from the Employees State Pension twisting words from robbed to misappropriate.

I am no lawyer but these are their words on their State page. How do you interpret them? Why is the State of Illinois not paying their bills, utilities, medical, bills at local gas stations?

We are only as great as the leader we follow.

Trump speaks to America   Busch speaks Busch

2016 presidential candidates are speaking out but what are they really saying let's listen to Donald Trump's speech and Jeb Busch's. We are in need of new blood, new leadership and I think the next president will have to be strong, relentless, smart and charismatic. I think he will have to be honest and transparent, like President Obama spoke of but never was.

One of these two will stand out for a variety of reasons. Both will show their true colors, as they speak to America and try to gain your support. One thing these two candidates have in common is name recognition.

If you are ready we will get started, as we listen to Donald Trump first, and then Jeb Busch. 2016 will be here before you know it.

Donald Trump's presidential speech

"Thank you very much everybody. So this began with five hundred people in a ball room in Phoenix. The hotel called us up and said please don't do it here we're going to be swamped and you're going to destroy the building. It's been amazing, sadly we have thousands of people that can't get in. So you know real estate, you know real estate.

I want to thank everyone, last night you actually saw it on television it was carried live. We had an amazing, an amazing event, a very sad event and yet very beautiful. Because the word is getting out we have to stop illegal immigration, we have to. We have a situation that is absolutely out of control.

We have incompetent politicians, not only the president. I mean right here in your own State. You have John McCain. I just hate to see when people don't have common sense or don't have an understanding of what is going on, or perhaps don't want to know, maybe it's campaign contributions, maybe it's special interests, maybe it's lobbyists, but for some reason they don't get it. I doubt they will be in office much longer.

We are going to make this country so great again. We are going to work, we are going to work so hard. When we had are event last night I saw hardened veteran reporters who were crying, you got to see this people that I have known for a long time people I don't even like, they're not good people."

"How you doing back there?" as he looks behind him at the crowd as the crowd roars and starts clapping. "One in particular, tears streaming down his face. I don't believe what I am saying. I didn't think he had a tear in him. Some of the people that spoke were absolutely amazing. One, their child was killed by an illegal immigrant, who shouldn't have been here.

This really began for me, it's very interesting, because when I started, and when I announced , now don't forget they said he's never going to go run, right. Then they said very strongly, now these people are very knowledgeable, now they don't know anything. Then they said he'll never file his FEC paper. I filed that two weeks ago, they said, "Oh wow." Then they said he'll never file his financials, cause he is not as rich as people think. I will be filing later this week, and by the way other candidates will not be filing from what I hear. When I filed the number was actually much higher than anybody knew, and I am not saying that to brag I am only saying that because that is the kind of thinking we need to be thinking . Where trade deals with China, with Japan, with India, with everybody.

We are getting ripped we are being taken apart piece by piece slowly, slowly. China laughs at us, they laugh at our stupidity. They laugh at our incompetent politicians. They have geniuses negotiating for them, we have people that don't have a clue, they don't have a clue.

Mexico and by the way I have only said this about two hundred times, but it never gets reported. I love the Mexican people, I love the spirit of the Mexican people.

I love them. Many, many people from Mexico legal, they went in the old fashion way, they're legal. Many, many people from Mexico work for me. Over the years thousands of Hispanics have worked for me. Many of them work for me now, but thousands, they're incredible people. By the way nobody ever says that. They always cut that part out. I'll go a step further, I respect Mexico as a country, but the problem we have is that their leaders are much smarter, much sharper, and much more cunning then our leaders. They are killing us at the border, and they are killing us in trade, They are killing us. Every once in a while I will see a rally and it's put up by the Mexican government in my opinion. People come in and they are so perfect they are like central casting. You know how long the rallies last, like about twelve minutes. They go home

I have heard this many times, it is very hard as a successful person to run for president. I have heard this from the time i was a little boy to run for president, or even for political office. I find it, I have headlines every day. ESPN drops Trump.

A friend of mine in Paris called and said, "Oh Don it's too bad about ESPN." Do you know what they were doing? They rented my golf club for the day. They put up a big deposit I took their deposit and rented it to somebody else. I made two for the price of one. Then the next day all over the world NASCAR drops Trump, no NASCAR,NASCAR and then friends of mine call up from Europe. Headlines NASCAR. Don it's too bad about NASCAR I feel so. Do you know what that one was? They rented a banquet hall at Trump National in Miami. I took their deposit."

He motions his hands as though it is obvious what he did doubling his money. "I took their deposit and you know what I just rented it for much more than they were paying. Two for the price of one. You know I might make money running for president, it's very interesting. Then all over the place I hear Macy's, now Macys hurts a little bit because the head of Macy's is a great friend of mine, Terry Lundgren. Nice guy, he called me up and I am in New Hampshire, and I am getting ready to go on to make a speech. It's sort of interesting, it's like six thirty in the evening and I get a call from Terry Lundgren from Macys. The speech is packed, it's like a house it's supposed to be in the house. They didn't have enough room they had three or four hundred people and they never thought this was going to happen. They thought there was going to be thirty, like this. This is a little larger, but the same thing proportionately.

So my phone rings it's Terry Lundgren of Macys and the man on the stage is getting ready to introduce me, and he says you know we have Donald Trump the American dream, blah, blah, blah. The phone rings during the introduction, I am going to be going up there in less than a minute. He says Donald hi. He is like my best friend, I said Terry what's the problem? He says your very controversial." Donald Trump holds up his hands as what's the problem? The crowd roars as they all start clapping and whistling. He says, now I am suppose to be going up I have a speech. I have all these people. By the way cameras live cameras all over the place just like you got here. He said he got calls from Hispanic people saying they are going to boycott Macys, I don't know what to do?

I said Terry be tough. They will be gone, one day, one day. Now this is a guy I played golf with I'm with him all the time really, cause I don't forget things. I don't forget things. He said please Donald can I cut you? It's not a big deal I'm selling ties and you know what honestly they were made in China so I didn't care that much.

So I am walking up the stairs to make a speech and I have Lundgren saying I like to cut you, because he is going to get some bad publicity, he thinks. I walk up stairs I hear them say and now the American dream and I am still talking to Lundgren. It's like a minute and a half before I walk on the stage and people say what happened?

I made a good speech no notes no nothing. Everybody was happy, and I just got cut from Macys and here is the bottom line on Macys. Thousands and thousands of people are cutting up their Macys credit cards.

Thousands, then I get a call from NBC, now let me tell you about NBC. No, no I got to tell you. Now look I love the people at NBC. We had a tremendous success with the Apprentice, and they renewed the Apprentice, see I give up a lot. You are going to see how much money I made with the Apprentice come Wednesday, or Thursday when I do my filing. Seriously it's a very lucrative, you know it's great when you have a big television show it's like you're a movie star you get a lot of money right. Not that much but a lot. You are going to see very impressive numbers, so NBC calls they would like to see me.

Now they don't care about inclusion, they were talking about inclusion. You know they write the press release. So I read this, this is incredible. They call me and a couple of months ago the head of NBC comes to see me, and the head of NBC's boss. I don't want to mention any names because they are really good friends of mine, although I will probably never speak to them again either.

You know the head of NBC is COMCAST they own NBC. I get a call from NBC the head of reality, the head president of NBC, and the head of everything, COMCAST. They come to see me." "Please do the Apprentice." "I say I can't I want to make America great again. I have done the Apprentice now for twelve years, and it's a great show.

For twelve years there has been fourteen or fifteen copies of the Apprentice, everyone has failed, every single one. I could give you the names but I don't want to embarrass the people, ah I'll give you a couple names. Nice people Mark Cuban did one called the Benefactor. The Benefactor was a disaster. Richard Branson did one great guy, but he did one, it didn't work out. Tommy Hilfiger who I love tented my building great guy didn't work out. Hiltons did one, Martha Stewart did one for us, did one for Mark Burnett and Donald Trump.

Martha Stewart, she just got out of the can, no it's true. She's hot as a pistol. You know they show her coming out in the whole outfit she is wearing. I'm thinking what a great deal. So we actually did a show by us called the Apprentice. Within a couple weeks it was over, so I must have something right?

So here's the story. NBC sees us, they're smart people. NBC comes to my office and they want me to do the Apprentice so badly, and what do I do? I say I can't I'm going to run for president. I can't because of equal time a stupid law. Obama can go on television all day long and be president and run for office, but if I have a television show, what happens is everybody that is running for office would have to be able to do the Apprentice show equal time. So you will have a good guy Rick Santorum, you will have all these guys.

You will have someone that used to head up Lehman Brothers, the governor from Ohio. The Lehman Brothers almost took down the world. He was a managing partner. He is a nice man, I don't know him, but I know if you are the managing partner of Lehman Brothers, you're not looking to good. All of these guys would have to be given two hours of prime time television on Sunday or Monday night, I don't think so.

So they came to my office told me they would like me to do it, so important. Wait they renewed the Apprentice. It was really very interesting cause a lot of people said how could they do this? They announce the Apprentice which is good cause I always want to be loved, you know?

Like if I went on dates and a woman dropped me, which happened often. I would like to say I dropped her So what happened is the renewed the Apprentice and I said I wasn't going to do it, because I am going to run for president. They didn't believe me. I said why don't you believe me? They say why would you give up a primetime show? Mark Burnett calls from Survivor, a great guy, he really is and a friend of mine.

He calls Donald they're giving you an extension, nobody turns down an extension. He said I never heard of it before. I said Mark I am going to run for president, nobody believed me. Then I run and the guys in my office say run and then by September we'll do something. Can you believe that. Well if I don't do well I would have done that, you know if it's not doing well why not. There is a problem, we just went to number one in the polls.

So NBC went nuts, they renewed their show and they don't have their star and everybody else failed with similar shows. NBC is angry with me so again don't believe the inclusion they got Reverend Al Sharpton working for them. Ok He's actually not a bad guy he's a conman, you have to understand that. He is a conman says I'm going to pick at you if you don't give, he is a conman. I have known him over twenty years they got Lying Brian Williams, he's ok.

They sent me the most beautiful present a few months ago. I shouldn't tell you the name but Titleist golf balls, They sent me hundreds and hundreds of Titleist golf balls, they sent them to me. On the card From your friends at NBC. A short time later they say he's not inclusive, me, I am more inclusive than anybody. I then get a call from Univision. Now Univision controls. Univision has a certain power, now I didn't know much about Univision. I thought they were very wealthy, actually they're not very wealthy at all. They are highly over levered. They got like ten billion dollars in debt. They have to do an IPO, now how stupid is this. They could have waited a couple of weeks did their IPO and been done, instead they do it early they couldn't do it fast enough.

Because you know why, it's strictly my opinion but the Mexican government totally tells Univision which is 80% of the market 70% totally what to do, totally. So the Mexican government is not happy with me to put it bluntly and again I respect Mexico but their leaders are too smart for our leaders, we have stupid leaders ok.

I'll tell you just between you and I, just between this little group." " Thank you very much," as he comments back to a group in the back of the crowd. Trump saying USA, USA as he smiles toward the small crowd of Mexican supporters. The Mexican government doesn't care about the border nearly as much as it cares about the bad trade deals America is making with Mexico, that's really what it's all about. So I just sued Univision for five hundred million dollars.

With all of that being said, we have to be strong. We have to take our country back. We have to run the country properly. I am going to bring up a man who is a great man. He is a great, great guy. I saw him the other day on television." " It's ok you can shout." "Because I'm telling you about the bad deals this countries making. Mexico I respect the country, they're taking our jobs, they're taking our manufacturing, they're taking our money, they're taking everything and they are killing us on the borders and Mexico does not like it, so remember this." "Don't worry we will take our country back, very soon." The crowd start shouting USA, USA, USA, as it once again quiets for Donald Trump."So the other day, it's funny I got a great review including my opening speech when I announced I was running for president.

It wasn't till five days later people started saying, oh he said something, what they don't say is they cut it in the middle of the sentences. They cut it because those people not all of them, some of them are great, but many of them are very dishonest people, meaning the press. Very dishonest, very dishonest.

I'll give you one quick example because I want to bring somebody up here for a second. I say and it's fairly standard, cause I believe in it strongly. The American dream is dead but I am going to make it bigger and stronger and better than ever, right. I say it every once in a while I won't, but I don't use teleprompters like the president I speak from the heart. So I say the American dream is dead, I am going to make it bigger and better. So I go home my wife says darling that was such a tough statement. I said what? I turn on the television and I see the American dream is dead period cut. I said oh what a horrible statement. They are so dishonest.

You know what I usually do, because if you really love this country you have a very, very hard time convincing people that what you are doing is right, and that what you are doing is smart. Like a lot of us are smart, I'm really smart I went to the Horton school of finances did well made a fortune. Wrote a book called the *Art of the deal*, everybody read that book? They say the number one selling business book of all time, I'll say one of them because if I am slightly off by two copies they'll say Trump exaggerated, but I think it was the number one best seller.

I wrote many number one best sellers, many, I think twelve. I did a lot of things but the *Art of the deal* was the number one business book of all time. Great then I do the Apprentice , became this tremendous hit NBC was desperate to have, now they got to put somebody else in there we'll see how long it lasts. Then I hear Donald Trump doesn't deserve to be on some stage with some failed Senator, failed Governor, or failed something, kind of amazing isn't it. The poll just came out and it said I am tied with Jeb bush, I said that's too bad. How can I be tied with this guy he's terrible, he's terrible. He's weak on immigration. You know the sanctuary cities, you know the sanctuary cities he had five of them in Florida while he was Governor. Did you know that, I didn't know that.

He is totally in favor of common core, meaning your children in Phoenix and other places are going to be educated by bureaucrats from Washington who for the most part just want to pick up a check, give me a break.

He is in support of that I don't see him as a factor. I know it is the Busch name which got us into, well in fairness not the greatest. But Jeb Busch I don't get it, so when they said Mr. Trump you are in first place you're tied with Jeb Busch. That's not good how can I be tied with Jeb Busch. I'm going to bring someone up to say just a few words, his son was viciously and violently shot by an illegal immigrant. His son was a star athlete, a star student, he applied to Stanford and many great colleges. He would have been and could have gone anywhere. I met Jemel about a week ago I see this guy, he's mentioning my name. I say oh no not again thinking he is killing me like everybody else.

My wife says no I think he is saying good things. I said I doubt it they're hitting me left and right. I turn up the television and hear the only man sticking up for us is Donald Trump. He introduces Mr. Shaw You can see the rest of his speech on You-tube.

Donald Trump spoke with passion and from his heart as he tried to share with us all, his ideas and goals. He spoke about illegal immigration and didn't waffle fearing he might offend someone. He stood tall and was open and honest about his views on illegal immigration. He was the first to acknowledge the problem with solutions.

Donald Trump is definitely charismatic. He has stated he is not going to take money from the Lobbyists and special interests groups. He pointed out the incompetent politicians we currently have in office, you don't even have to look hard with President Obama and ex Secretary of State Hillary Clinton. While President Obama spoke of transparency putting more windows in the White House he was ordering more curtains and blinds to shield us from the truth. Sure this part is just sarcasm on the transparency issue.

The truth is with transparency it all starts with being honest, not afraid to show your hand and keep your hand. Many politicians like to only show part of their hand while they want you to believe what the rest of the cards they are holding are what they tell you, not show you. This is called politics but in my world it is called deception.

Now it is Jeb Busch's turn to talk to us, are you ready?

Jeb Busch presidential speech.

Thank you all very much. Thank you for that great introduction. I have had a blast these last twenty four hours in New Hampshire. You all know how to be a magnet to candidates. There are only about fifty five people running for president as best I can tell. We're probably going to be a driver for creating highway jobs for New Hampshire, which I want to play my part in today, so thank you for letting me come.

Everybody knows me as George's boy, Barbra's boy, W's brother. I have some other family members but if I am going to go beyond the consideration of running for the highest office in the land, I need to share a little bit of my heart to show my life experience.

For those of you that have family members I think you can appreciate this, we are not always like our brother and sister, or our mom and dad. We all have our own unique DNA and our own life experiences. While I am blessed my eyes opened up in the middle of Texas. My eyes opened up and there she was, the greatest mom I could ever imagine. I didn't know it at the time, but I, it turns out I won the lottery. I wish everybody could of had the upbringing that I had with two beautiful parents. I love them with my heart and soul.

My life began, my transformation began when I was in Mexico at the age of seventeen on a Sunday afternoon where I met my wife, literally she was in a car, I was sitting on the town square and our eyes met and I fell madly in love with her, it was love at first sight.

For the young guys here it does happen. Trust me and my life was organized in a way I cannot describe to you from there on end. It wasn't love at first sight for my wife sadly. In fact it took her a couple years to get going. Some of you may have had that experience, but she finally consented and we've been together forty one years.

We got married in Austin Texas. I just turned twenty one she was twenty. I got out of the University of Texas in two and a half years, and I started my life journey with her. It has been a great ride. We have lived in Venezuela for two years. We moved back I worked on my dad's campaign, I started my life in Miami as a business person. Before I mention, I forgot to mention three other people, those are my three kids. Jeb was my business partner He lives in Miami he has two great granddaughters and a wonderful wife. My daughter Noel lives in Orlando. My son George p. Some of you may know him is a State wide elected Official. He lives in Texas. I am incredibly proud of P. And Mandy, they actually brought a baby in to the world four days ago.

So as I begin to think about this journey, little Georgia, little Vinnie, little P. We call him Prescott and Jack. What is the world going to look like for them? Is it going to be a world of purpose and abundance, or is it going to be a world of great insecurity and fear where people feel compelled to not dream the biggest possible dreams, or they sit back and wonder what it's like that uncertainty makes it harder for all of us to rise up. My personal belief is that this is the greatest time to be alive as Americans. My son by the way served he volunteered at the age of thirty to serve in the Navy Reserves. He was an intelligence Officer and served in Afghanistan.

I'm proud of all of his life but I'm particularly proud of that, and I'm proud of the men and women here in New Hampshire and across the country who have served our country to keep us free. It's an obligation to all of us to pay our respect to them by giving them the best care they deserve in our Veterans department, And also honor them by keeping America strong, so their sacrifice was not in vain.

I did something when I started my journey as an adult, I actually learned how to sign the front side of a paycheck. I built a business with my friend Armando Perdina. It started with three people and went into the largest full service real estate company in South Florida. It got up to about 260 to 280 people.

It doesn't work the way the Progressive Liberals in Washington want to believe. We all just have to march one step forwards, one step forwards, back and forth do what you are told, that's not America. America looks like the life journey of many of the people in this room. It's dynamic where you take risks where it doesn't always work out, where you may have a failure but you dust yourself off.

In the interaction of all of us in pursuit of our own unique dreams in a free society has created a greatness of society, not the top down driven approach of the Liberals, and I have learned it by doing it. I think it's important, in fact if I had to pick what I valued the most out of my life experience that makes me feel confident that future looks bright is exactly what I said, signing the front side of a paycheck. Growing Jobs, having the challenges that we address in the real world.

I got to be governor of the State of Florida, some of you may know. Some of you may go secretly down there in January and February. I know I've seen you on the streets of Miami, Tampa and other places.

It's an incredible State. It's big, it's dynamic, it's kind of wacky, kind of crazy. Definitely purple, it's definitely purple. It's a State that I got to apply conservative principles, in a way to move the needle for people to have a better life. I did it with diligence, I did it with passion, I did it with conviction and the State is better off because we shifted towards a conservative philosophy, not just talking about it we did it.

In Florida when I was governor I said we needed to cut taxes other than raise taxes. I never raised taxes in my 8 years. We cut taxes every year. 19 billion dollars of cumulative tax cuts back in the pockets of people who then could pursue their dreams as they see fit.

We reduced the State's work force by 13,000 people, more than ten percent. Not many States can make that claim particularly a State that was growing like Florida. We rebuilt our reserves. This sounds like a nerdy thing I guess, but reserving for a rainy day is what conservatives do, spending money you don't have is what liberals do.

In Florida we reserved for a rainy day. We started with a billion dollars, when I left we had 9.5 billion dollars in reserves. The net result by the way was during that 8 years we were the only State to go from **double A** to **triple A** bond rating.

It used to be the bond agencies would look at the States and say you have to tax everything, have an excuse me for living tax, tax the air you breathe tax. The broad base tax code would generate the most solvent kind of State.

We went to the bond rating agencies and said no, no, what we need is a dynamic State of limited government, where economy grows, where income grows faster than the size and scope of government, in doing so you create a more solvent State and they rewarded us the only State to go up to triple A bond rating.

We took on the trial bar, if anybody has tried that it's a big challenge. We took them on to find a balanced approach to our ports system so the uncertainty was made better. We did something that was important, I don't know how it is in New Hampshire, but in Florida we had the second highest premiums for workers compensation, it was a huge driver for lessoning the opportunity for job growth.

We reformed it by taking on those that were making a lot of money on the system, and we created 400 million dollars a year reduction in premiums. I guarantee you that money went into the hands of small businesses and then out so those businesses could expand and jobs were created.

I was called Veto Corlioni, actually I was called a lot of things particularly by those on the left in my State, they didn't quite agree with everything that we did.

I was called Veto Corlioni, because I vetoed 2,500 separate line items in the budget totaling 2 billion dollars bringing order to a budget process which allowed personal income to grow at about four and a half percent, and government income to grow at about two and a half percent and the net result was, that we created 1.3 million net new jobs in Florida during my 8 years second only to California and 5 out of those 8 we lead the nation in job growth. We did other things as well, we eliminated affirmative action by executive order.

We replaced it with a leadership model that did not discriminate by race, but applied leadership principles which allowed for more minorities to, that were qualified to attend our universities.

During my 8 years more Hispanics and more African Americans attended our university, but during my 8 years we did not use a system that discriminated from one group to another.

We affirmed and expanded second Amendment rights, gun rights in our State. I think if you look at Florida you will see Florida is a model for the Second Amendment. We defend it, we defend the sanctity of life from beginning to end in our State, and we reform the things that are most important. My set of values believes that the most vulnerable should be in the front of the line, not in the back of the line. Republicans do better when they show their consciousness to do the exact same, whether the Veteran disabled, or the child welfare system, or the people who are struggling.

We should give them the attention and the help, reform the systems to make sure we have a better chance to rise up and in Florida I do believe more and more people have had a chance to rise up, because we reformed our education system like nobody's business.

In Florida we were languishing near the bottom, or at the bottom. In fact we were fiftieth in graduation rate when I started this journey, by expanding school choice the most dramatic expansion of any State in the country.

We were the first State with a State wide voucher program, we expanded the corporate tax scholarship program that has begun here with a baby step and we have 70,000 students that are taking advantage of that.

We are the first State to have a voucher program for kids who have a learning disability' where their parents can send them to private options. We have the largest number of kids attending a virtual school in the country. We eliminated social promotion in third grade.

That may not sound like a big deal but that is an insidious policy in our country. It is shameful that we have a policy that says a third grader going into fourth grade that it's ok that they are functioning illiterate. Moms know this and dads know this, that if you can't read by the third grade you are not going to acquire knowledge. In most places we don't have the courage to take on the teachers unions, bureaucracy both focused on the economic interests of the adults, rather than moving to a child center system where their God given abilities can learn.

The net result of turning the system upside down with high standards with robust accountability, with accurate assessments with school choice was that Florida has been the leader in regards to leaning gains in the United States of America.

I am proud of that, it's not like Washington's going to be the next place where the president ends up being the head of a school board, that is not what I am advocating, God forbid if that were to happen. It is important rather than just talking about things. I think it is important to look at peoples records. What have they done? Have they moved the needle? Have they the courage of their convictions? Have they focused on making sure everybody has a chance to rise up?

We are moving into a world, we are at an intersection, we are either going to be in a decline, because we refuse to change the things that are broken, or on the verge of the greatest time to be alive.

If you think about it today we are challenged we are in a sixth year of recovery but most Americans think we are still in a recession and they are. We are in a sixth year recovery but business starts up rates are lower than business failure rates and that's a challenge. We are in the sixth year of a so called recovery and work force participation rates and business participation rates, business startup rates are lower than they were in 1980.

I know we can do better, in fact it has to be done better and we can do better, but it requires the type of leadership that creates strategy of high sustained economic growth, where more and more people have a chance at earned success. That is how we will win, we will win if we offer a hopeful compelling alternative grounded in principle, using applied commonsense leadership to fix things.

We are in a verge, my little 4 year old, my 4 day old Jack is going to live till he is 130 years old. Your kids and grandkids are going to as well. We're on a verge of discovering cures of diseases , using life science in a way that defies our imagination. Every sector of our economy is being transformed with disruptive technologies and innovations. The question that we have in front of us is are we capable of making disruption our friend or will it over whelm us?

That requires leadership to fix a few complex things. None of this is possible unless we restore a sense of security in America. A sense of security that is based on the American leadership in the world. This is the first president in the post World War II era that does not believe that Americas presence in the world as a leader and the power in the world as a force for good, I do and I hope you do as well.

We need to re-nourish the alliances that have kept us safe. We need a president that does not disrespect our friends like Israel and tries to cater to our enemies, like Iran.

We need a president that doesn't unilaterally give away things, but negotiates on principle and strength, and is engaged where our friends know we have their back, not just today but over the long haul and our enemies fear us again. That is how you create a more secure and stable world.

So if we do those two things where we grow our economy at a rate that our people no longer believe that the end is near, that their children will have more opportunities than they had. That they are willing to take risks again and that we build capacity so that everybody has an opportunity at earned success. That we advocate a strong America a presence in the world that creates a greater security than what we have today, this will be the greatest time to be alive.

I hope you agree with that and hope you will support the candidates and people that have this hopeful and optimistic vision, because that is how we will win as well.

I know in fact we will not win if we just complain about how things are. What we have to do is be principle in our opposition from the statuesque for sure, but we also have to offer a compelling alternative, so that more, and more, and more people join us in our cause. Thank you all for letting me join you and allowing me to come."

Let's look at his speech for a moment and see what he really let us know about himself. Is he being real or is he just another politician?

He starts his speech off strategically as he informs the world Who he is. He is the son to former President George Busch and Barbra Busch, his brother is W. Busch. He wants us to know him for who he is, playing both sides of the field which is smart on his part. Trying to collect the supporters of the Busch name while collecting those who will see him as his own individual, or those who oppose the Busch legacy. He tries to separate himself in a manner of political ecstasy.

It is interesting how he forgot about his kids and then when he remembered them spoke of how proud he was of his boys while he skimmed over his daughter Noel who lives in Orlando, Florida She has a criminal past with drugs. Why didn't he mention that as well and talk about his love for his daughter even if she has made poor choices. He could of used that to relate to the many who's parents have had children that have done drugs, or even a small crime. It is typical of a politician to only present the good side just like in a debate where you argue your point, while clouding the waters making your opponents defense murky.

It is time to move on to the Republican debate and see where our candidates wish to take us. Are you ready?

CHAPTER FIVE

The first Republican debate covered by Fox News on August 6, 2015. It was covered live and millions from around the world watched, now that I don't know but I watched. Let's get ready to watch the debate live here for the first time between the pages of Changing America 2016.

"Gentlemen we know how much you like hand raising questions, so we promise this is the only one tonight, the only one. Is there any one on stage, and can I see hands tonight who is unwilling to pledge support to the eventual nominee of the Republican party and pledge to not run an independent campaign against that person. Again we are looking for you to raise your hand now if you won't make that pledge tonight."

Donald Trump immediately put his hand up signifying he would not make that pledge tonight. He did not look both ways so as to waffle depending on the other candidates.

He stood tall on his belief. Once again remember we are looking for the next President to lead us to triumph and prosperity.

"Mr. Trump to be clear you are standing on a Republican primary stage."

"I fully understand that."

"The place where the R and C will give the nominee the nod."

"I fully understand." Donald repeats.

"Experts say that an independent run would almost certainly hand the run over to Democrats and likely another Clinton. You cannot say tonight that you can make that pledge?"

" I cannot say, I have to respect that person if they win if it's not me, if I do win and I'm leading by quite a bit and that's what I want to do. I can totally make that pledge if I am the nominee. I pledge I would not run as an independent, but I am talking about it with everybody. We are talking about a lot of leverage. We want to win and we will win. I want to win as the Republican nominee."

Senator Rand Paul interrupts. "This is what's wrong he buys and sells politicians of all stripes. He is already hedging his bet on the Clintons, so if he doesn't run as a Republican Maybe he supports Clinton or maybe he runs as an Independent. I'd say he's already hedging his bets to the Clintons because he is used to buying politicians."

"I have given you plenty of money." Donald Trump responds to Senator Rand Paul.

"So to be clear you are not going to make the pledge tonight?"

"I will not make the pledge at this time."

"Gentlemen our first round of questions are on the grounds of electability in the general election and we start tonight with you, Doctor Carson. You are a successful Neurosurgeon, but you admit that you had to study up when it comes to foreign policy saying there is a lot to learn. Your critics say that your inexperience shows. You suggested the Baltic States are not a part of NATO. And just months ago you were unfamiliar with the political parties in government in Israel and domestically you thought Allen Greenspan was Treasury Secretary instead of Federal Reserve Chair. Aren't these basic mistakes and don't they raise legitimate concerns about whether or not you are ready to be President?"

"Well I could take issue with all of those things, but we don't have time, but I will say we have a debate here tonight and we will have an opportunity to explore those areas and I am very much looking forward to demonstrating that in fact , the thing that is probably most important is having a brain.

To figure things out and learn things very rapidly. You know experience comes from a large area of different arenas and America became a great nation early on, not because America was flooded by politicians, but because it was flooded with people that understood the value of personal responsibility, hard work, creativity and a innovation and that is what will get us on the right track now."

"Senator Rubio when Jeb Bush announced his candidacy for president, he said this "There is no passing off responsibility as governor, no blending in to the legislative crowd." Could you please address Governor Busch and explain to him across the stage here, why someone like you who has never held executive office. Why you are better prepared to be president then he is and that you said he did a great job running your State of Florida?"

"Let me begin by saying this, I'm not new to the political process. I was making contributions as the speaker of the third largest State in the country well before I got into the Senate. I would add to that, that this can't be about a resume competition. It is important to be qualified, but if this is a resume competition than Hillary Clinton is going to be the next president, because she has been in office and in government longer than anyone here tonight.

Here is what this election should be about. It should be about the future not the past. It better be about the issues our nation is facing today, not some of the issues we once faced. This country is facing an economy that's been radically transformed.

You know the largest retailer in the country today Amazon who doesn't even own a store. These changes have been disruptive. They have changed people's lives that once sustained our middle class, they either don't pay enough or they are gone. We need someone who understands that as our nominee.

If I am your nominee how is Hillary Clinton going to lecture me living paycheck to paycheck, I was raised paycheck to paycheck. How is she going to lecture me on student loans I owed over a hundred thousand dollars just four years ago. If I am our nominee we will be the party of the future."

"Governor Busch you have insisted that you are your own man. You say you have a life experience uniquely your own, not your father's, not your brother's, but there are some candidates on this stage that get big applause lines in early voting States with this line." "The last thing we need is another Busch in the Oval Office." "So do you understand the real concern in this country about dynastic politics?"

"Absolutely I do and I'm going to run hard, run with heart and run to win. I am going to have to earn this, maybe the barrier is set even higher for me, that's fine. I got a record in Florida. I am proud of my dad, and I'm certainly proud of my brother. In Florida they call me Jeb because I earned it. I cut taxes every year totaling 19 billion dollars, we balanced every budget. We went from 1 billion dollars of reserves to 9 billion dollars of reserves. We are one of two States that went to triple A bond rating. They call me Veto Colioni, because I vetoed 2500 separate line items in the budget.

I am my own man I govern conservative and I govern effectively. The net effect was that during my 8 years 1.8 million jobs were created. We left the State better off, because I applied conservative principles in a purple State the right way and people rose up.

"Mr. Trump one of the things people love about you is you speak your mind and you don't use a politicians filter, however that is not without its downsides, in particular when it comes to women. You've called women you don't like fat pigs, dogs, slobs, and disgusting animals. Your twitter account." Interruption.

"Only Rosie O'Donnell." Donald Smiles as he lets her finish. The crowd cheers.

"No it wasn't, your twitter account, for the record it was well beyond Rosie O'Donnell."

"Yes, I'm sure it was."

"Your twitter account has several disparaging comments about women's looks. You once told a contestant on Celebrity Apprentice it would be a pretty picture to see her on her knees. Does that sound to you like a temperament of a man we should elect president and how will you answer the charge when Hillary Clinton who is most likely going to be the Democratic nominee, that you are part of the war on women?"

"I think the big problem that this country has is being politically correct. I have been challenged by so many people and I don't have time for total political correctness and to be honest with you this country doesn't either.

This country is in big trouble, we don't win anymore. We lose to China, we lose to Mexico, both in trade and at the border. We lose to everybody. Frankly what I say and often It's fun, it's kidding we have a goodtime. What I say is what I say.

Honestly Megan if you don't like it, I'm sorry though I have been very nice to you though I could maybe not be based on the way you have treated me, but I wouldn't do that. You know what, we need strength, we need energy, we need quickness, and we need brains in this country to turn it around, that I can tell you right now."

"Senator Cruz, your colleague Senator Paul right next to you said a few months ago that he agrees with you on a number of issues, but that you do nothing to grow the party. He says you feed red meat to the base, but you don't reach out to minorities, you have a toxic relationship with GOP leaders in Congress, you even called the Republican Senate leader Mitch McConnell a liar recently. How can you win in 2016 if you are such a divisive figure?"

"Chris, I believe the American people are looking for someone to speak the truth. If you are looking for someone to go to Washington to go along to get along, to get along to agree with the career politicians of both parties, who get in bed with the lobbyist and special interests, then I am not your guy. There is a reason that we have 18 trillion dollars in debt, because as conservatives and Republicans we keep winning elections. We got a Republican House, we got a Republican Senate and we don't have leaders that honor their commitments. I will always tell the truth and do what I said I would do."

"Governor Christie, you are not exactly the darling of conservatives, you tout your record as a Republican governor in a blue State. On Face book the most people talking about you not surprisingly are from your State of New Jersey. One of the top issues they are talking about is the economy. This may be why, under your watch New Jersey has gone down 9 credit rating downgrades. The States 44th in private sector growth. You face an employee pension crisis and the garden State has the third largest foreclose rate in the country. So why should voters believe that your management of the country's finances be any different?"

"If you think they are bad now you should have seen it when I got there. The fact is the 8 years before I became governor, taxes and fees were raised at State level 115 times. In the 8 years before I got there spending was increased 56% and in the 8 years before I got there, there was zero net profit job growth in the private sector, zero.

What did we do, we came in and balanced the budget, 11 billion dollar deficit on a 29 billion dollar budget by cutting over 800 programs out of the State budget. We brought the budget in to balance with no tax increase, in fact we vetoed 5 income tax increases during my time as governor. We cut business taxes 2.3 billion dollars and we cut regulation by one third what my predecessor put in place, and what has happened since 192,000 new private sector new jobs in my five and a half years as governor.

We have a lot of work to do in New Jersey, but I am darn proud of how we brought our State back."

"Governor Walker you have consistently said you want to make abortion illegal even in the case of rape, incest, or to save the life of the mother. You recently signed an abortion law in Wisconsin that does have an exception for the mother's life, but you are on record as having objected to it.
Would you really let a mother die rather than have an abortion, and with 83% of the American public in favor of a life exception are you to out of the mainstream on this issue to win this election?"

"Well I am pro life, I have always been pro life and I got a position that is consistent with many Americans out there, in that I believe that is an unborn child in need of protection. I have said many of times that an unborn child should be protected and there are many alternatives out there to protect the life of the mother, that has been consistently proven. Unlike Hilary Clinton who has a radical view in terms of support for Planned Parenthood. I defunded Planned Parenthood more than 4 years ago, long before any of these videos came out. I've got a position that is in line with every day America."

"Governor Huckabee, like Governor walker you have staked out strong positions on social issues, you favor a Constitutional Amendment banning same sex marriages. You favor a Constitutional Amendment favoring abortions except for the life of the mother. Millions of people agree with you in this country, but according to the polls and this is an electability question and according to the polls more people don't, so how do you persuade enough Independents and Democrats to get elected in 2016?"

"Chris I disagree with the idea that the real issue is a Constitutional Amendment, that's a long and difficult process, I've actually taken a position that is boulder than that. A lot of people are talking about defunding Planned Parenthood as if that's a huge game changer.

I think it's time to do something even more bold. I think the next president ought to evoke the fifth and fourteenth Amendment to the Constitution, now that we know that a baby inside the mother's womb is a person at the moment of conception. The reason that we know is because of the DNA schedule that we have clear scientific evidence of.

This notion that we continue to ignore the individual of the person is a violation of that unborn child's fifth and fourteenth Amendment rights for due process and equal protection under the law. It's time we recognize the Supreme Court is not the Supreme being and we change the policy to be pro life and to protect children and rip up their body parts and sell them like they're parts to a Buick."

"Senator Paul you've recently blamed the rise of Isis on Republican Hawks, now you later said that statement you could have said it better, but the statement went on and you said quote, "Everything they've talked about in foreign policy they've been wrong on for the last twenty years. Why are you so quick to blame your own party?"

"First of all only Isis is responsible for the terrorism, only Isis is responsible for the depravity. What we do have to examine, is how we going to defeat Isis? I've got a proposal.

I am the leading voice in America for not arming the allies of Isis. I've been fighting in the midst of a lot of opposition from Hillary Clinton as well as some Republicans who wanted to send arms to the allies of Isis. Isis rides around in a billion dollars worth of Humvees. It's a disgrace we ought to stop it. We shouldn't fund our enemies for goodness sakes.

We didn't create Isis, Isis created themselves, but we can stop them and one way is by not funding them and by not arming them."

"Governor Kasich you chose to expand Medicaid in your State, unlike several other governors on this stage tonight and it is already over budget by some estimates costing tax payers an additional 1.4 billion dollars in just the first 18 months. You've defended your Medicaid expansion by invoking God, saying to skeptics when they arrive in Heaven Saint Peter isn't going to ask them how small they kept government, but what they have done for the poor. Why should Republican voters who generally want to shrink government believe you won't use your Saint Peter rational to expand every government program?"

"First of all Megan, President Reagan expanded Medicaid 3 or 4 times. Second Megan I had an opportunity to bring resources back to Ohio, to do what? To treat the mentally ill, 10,000 of them sit in our prisons. It cost $22,500.00 a year to keep them in prison. I would rather get them their medication so they could lead a decent life.

Secondly we are rehabbing the drug addicted 80% of our people in prisons have addiction served problems. We now treat them in the prisons, release them in the community, and the recidivism rate is 10% and everybody across this country knows that the tsunami of drugs is threatening their families, so we are treating them and getting them on their feet and finally the working poor.

Instead of them coming into the emergency room where it cost more and they're sicker and we end up paying . We brought a program in here to make sure people could get on their feet.

You know what, everybody has a right for their God given purpose, and finally Medicaid is growing at one of the lowest rates in the country and finally we went from 8 billion in the hole to 2 million in the black. We cut 5 billion in taxes and we've grown 350,000 jobs."

"Governor Busch you released a new plan this week on illegal immigration focusing on enforcement, which some suggests so you're not soft on that issue. I want to ask you about a statement you made last year on illegal immigrants, and here is what you said."

"They broke the law but it's not a felony, it's an act of love, it's an act of commitment to your family."

"Do you stand by that statement and do you stand by your support of earned legal status?"

"I do. I believe that the great majority of people coming here, have no other option. They want to provide for their family. We need to control our border. It's our responsibility who comes in, so I've written a book about this and this week I came up with a comprehensive strategy that really mirrored what we said in the book."

So did he write the book or were there others? He did say what **we** said. It is these type statements that the American people want to know. Deception starts at the mouth of the speaker and is swayed by those with ears that chose to listen. Let's get back to his answer.

We need to deal with e-verify, we need to deal with people who come with a legal Visa and over stay, we need to be much more strategic on how we deal with border enforcement, border security, we need to eliminate the sanctuary cities in this country. It is ridiculous and tragic. People are dying because of the fact that local governments are not following the federal law.

There is much to do and instead of talking about this as a wedge issue, which Barrack Obama has done now for six long years. The next president and I hope to be that president, will fix this once and for all so that we can turn this in to a driver for high sustained economic growth and there should be a path for earned legal status, not amnesty, earned legal status which mean you pay a fine and do many things over an extended period of time."

"Mr. Trump it has not escaped any body's notice, you say the Mexican government, the Mexican government is sending criminals, rapists, drug dealers across the border. Governor Busch has called those remarks extraordinarily ugly. I'd like you, your right next to him tell us, talk to him directly and say how you respond to that and you have repeatedly said you have evidence the Mexican government is doing this.

That you have evidence that you have refused or declined to share. Why not use this first Republican presidential debate to share your proof with the American people?"

"So if it weren't for me you wouldn't even be talking about illegal immigration Chris, you wouldn't even be talking about it. This was not a subject that was on anybody's mind until I brought it up at my announcement and I said Mexico is sending, except the reporters said because generally they're a dishonest lot generally speaking in the world of politics, they didn't cover my statement the way I said it. The fact is since then, many killings, murders, crime, drugs pouring in across the border, our money going out and drugs coming in. I said we need to build a wall and it has to be built quickly and I don't mind having a big beautiful door in that wall so that people can come into this country legally, but we need Jeb to build a wall. We need to keep illegal's out."

"Mr. Trump I will give you thirty seconds to answer my question on what evidence you have specific evidence that the Mexican government is sending criminals across the border?"

"Ok , border patrol, I was at the border last week. Border patrol people that I deal with, that I talk to, they say this is what's happening, because our leaders are stupid, our politicians are stupid and the Mexican government is much smarter, much sharper, much more cunning and they send the bad ones over because they don't want to pay for them, they don't want to take care of them. Why should they when the stupid leaders of the United States will do it for them and that's what's happening whether you like it or not."

"Governor Kasich I know you don't like to talk about Donald Trump, but I do want to ask you about the merit of what he just said. When he said that the American leaders are stupid, that the Mexican government is sending criminals, that we are being bamboozled is that an adequate response on illegal immigration?"

"Chris first of all I was just saying to Chris Christie, they say we're out spoken. We need to take lessons from Donald Trump if we're really going to learn it. Here is the thing about Donald Trump.

Donald Trump is hitting a nerve in this country, he is people are frustrated, they're fed up. They don't think the government is working for them and for people that want to just tune him out they are making a mistake.

Now he's got his solutions, some of us have other solutions. You know I balanced the budget when I was one of the chief architects when I was in Washington, hadn't been done since. I was a military reformer. I took the State of Ohio from an 8 billion dollar hole and 350,000 job loss to a 2 million dollar surplus and a gain of 350,000 jobs."

"Respectfully can we get back to immigration."

"My point is that we all have solutions. Mr. Trump is touching a nerve because people want the wall to be built. They want to see an end to illegal immigration, they want to see it, we all do, but we all have different ways of getting there and you're going to hear from all of us tonight on what our ideas are."

"Senator Rubio let me try this with you, is this as simple as our leaders are stupid, their leaders are smart and all these illegal's coming over are criminals?"

"Let me tell you. Let me set you straight on a couple things. The evidence is clear that the illegal's coming across the border are not from Mexico they are coming from Guatemala, El Salvador, Honduras, those countries are the source of the people that are now the majority."

Just a history note those countries are just south of Mexico, that's like referring to Texas and Oklahoma when we mention Kansas and Nebraska. Back to Senator Rubio's answer.

" I also believe we need a fence, the problem is if El Chapo builds a tunnel under the fence we need to deal with that too. That is why you need an E- verify system and an entry tracking system and all sorts of other things to prevent illegal immigration.

I agree with what Governor Kasich said. People are frustrated. This is the most generous country in the world when it comes to immigration. There are a million people a year who legally immigrate to the United States and people feel like they are being taken advantage of. Despite our generosity people feel we are being taken advantage of and let me tell you about what never gets talked about in these debates.

People that call my office, who have been waiting for fifteen years to come here to the United States and they paid their fees and they hired a lawyer and they can't get in and they are wondering whether they should come here illegally and so these are important issues we should address.

It needs to be addressed, otherwise we will be talking about this for the next 30 years like we have for the last 30 years."

"Governor Walker from 2002 to as recently as 2013 just 2 years ago you supported comprehensive immigration reform, including a path to citizenship, now you say that was a quick reaction to something you hadn't really thought about and that you have changed your mind.

Other than politics could you explain why in the last 2 years you have changed your decision on a path to citizenship and I know there are other past decisions we should hold you to?"

"Chris I actually said it earlier on your show I acknowledged that. I actually listened to the American people and I think the American people actually want a leader that is going to listen to them. I talked to border State governors and other elected officials, I looked at how this President particularly through this last November messed up the immigration system in this country, more importantly I listened to the people of America. I believe we need to secure America.

I've been to the border with the Texas governor, Governor Abbott and others seeing the problems they have there.

There are international criminal organizations penetrating the Southern based borders and we need to do something about it. Secure the border, enforce the law, no amnesty and go forward with the legal immigration system that gives priorities to American working families and wages."

Senator Cruz some 1400 people submitted questions on this very hot topic on illegal immigration. On Face Book a number of them were about the murder of Kate Steinley of San Francisco and allegedly shot down by an illegal. Will you support Steinley's Law which will impose a 5 year minimum prison term for illegal's deported and returns to this country and will you defund sanctuary cities for violating federal law?"

"Chris absolutely yes, and not only will I support it, I have authored Kate's Law in the United States Senate and have filed that legislation. I tried to get the Senate to pass Kate's Law on the floor of the senate just one week ago and the leader of our own party blocked to vote on Kate's Law.

There was a reference made about our leaders being stupid. It's not a question of stupidity, it's that they don't want to enforce the immigration law. There are far too many in the Washington cartel that support amnesty.

President Obama talked about fundamentally transforming this country. There are 7 billion people across the face of the globe, many of whom want to come to this country legally great, but if they come illegally and they get amnesty, that is how we fundamentally change the country and it really is striking. A majority of candidates on this stage have supported amnesty I haven't. I never supported amnesty and I led the fight against Chuck Schumer's gang of amnesty legislation."

"Gentlemen we are going to switch topics now a bit and talk about terror and national security. Governor Christie you said Senator Paul's opposition of the NSA collection of phone records has made the United States weaker and more vulnerable, even going so far as being called before congress to answer for it. If we should be hit by another terrorist attack.

Do you really believe you can assign blame to Senator Paul just for opposing the bulk collection of peoples phone records in the case of another terrorist attack?"

"Yea, yes I do and I'll tell you why. I am the only person on the stage who has actually filed applications under the Patriot Act. Who has gone before the Federal Foreign Intelligence Court. Who has prosecuted, investigated, jailed terrorists in this country after September 11th. I was appointed US Attorney by President Bush on September 10, 2001 and the world changed enormously the next day and it happened in my State. It is not theoretical to me. I went to the funerals, we lost friends in the Trade Center that day. My own wife was two blocks from the Trade Center that day at her office having gone through it earlier that morning. When you actually have to be responsible for doing this, you can do it and we did it for seven years in my office, respecting civil liberties and protect the homeland.

I will make no apologies ever for protecting the lives and the safety of the American people. We need to get more tools to our folks to do that, not fewer and trust those people and oversee them to do it the right way, as president that is exactly what I will do."

Senator Rand Paul comments. "I want to collect more records from terrorists and less records from innocent Americans. The fourth Amendment is what we fought the Revolution over John Anderson said it was the spark that led to war for our independence and I am proud to be standing for the Bill of Rights, and I will continue to stand for the Bill of Rights."

Governor Christie responds. "Megan that is completely a ridiculous answer, I want to collect more records from terrorists, but less records from other people. How are you supposed to know Megan?"

Senator Paul again interrupts. "Use the fourth Amendment, use the fourth Amendment. Get a warrant, get a judge to sign it."

Listen Senator when you are sitting in a subcommittee just blowing hot air about this, you can say things about that. When you are responsible for saving the lives of the American people, then what you need to do is make sure you use the system the way you are suppose to."

"Here is the problem Senator, the Bill of Rights. Every time you got a case you got a warrant from a judge, I'm talking about searches without warrants. Indiscriminately of all Americans records and that's what I fought to end. I don't trust President Obama with our records. I know you gave him a big hug and if you want to give him a big hug go right ahead."

"You know Senator Paul the hugs I remember, are the hugs I gave to the families who lost their people on September 11 2001, those are the hugs I remember and those had nothing to do with politics unlike what you're doing by cutting speeches on the Senate floor then putting them on the internet in a half hour to raise money for your campaign while still putting our country at risk."

Megan asks a new question. "I want to get to a face book questioner whose name is Alex Sheldon and he has the following question.

"How will the candidates stop the treacherous actions of Isis, Isle and its strong influence in the US. If they were to become president?"

"Senator Cruz I want to talk to you about this because many of the Face Book users and the folks on Face Book wanted the candidates to speak to Isis tonight.

You asked the Chairman for the Joint Chiefs, a question. What would it take to destroy Isis in 90 days? He said they will only be truly destroyed once they are destroyed by the population in which they hide and then you accused him of pushing Medicaid for the Iraqi's. How would you destroy Isis in 90 days?"

"Megan we need a Commander in Chief that speaks the truth. We will not defeat radical Islamic terrorism so long as we have a president that will not utter the words **Radical Islamic Terrorism**.

When I asked General Dempsey Chairman of the Joint Chiefs, what would be required to destroy Isis militarily he said, There is no military solution, we need to change the conditions on the ground so that young men are not in poverty and susceptible to radicalization. That with all due respect is nonsense. It's the same answer the State Department gave, that we need to give them jobs. What we need is a Commander in Chief who makes clear if you join Isis if you wage jihad on America then you are signing your death warrant."

"You don't see it as an ideological problem vs. a military one?"

"Megan of course it is an ideological problem, that's why I introduced the Ex Patriot Act in the Senate, that said if any American traveled to the middle east and joins Isis then he or she forfeit their citizenship so they don't use a passport to come back and wage Jihad on Americans. Yes it is Ideological and let me contrast. President Obama who was at the prayer breakfast essentially acted as an apologist. He said well gosh the crusade the inquisitions. We need a president that shows the courage that Egypt's president shows, a Muslim when he called out the Radical Islamic Terrorists who were threatening the world."

"Governor Busch, for days on end on this campaign you struggled to answer a question about whether knowing what we do now would you still have invaded Iraq and Isis is now thriving there. You finally said no. To the families and soldiers that died in that war who say they liberated a country and deposed a ruthless dictator. How do you look at them now and tell them your brothers war was a mistake?"

"Knowing what we do now having faulty intelligence and not having security be the first priority when we invaded it was a mistake.

I wouldn't have gone in. However for the people that did lose their lives and the families that suffered I know this full well, because as Governor of the State of Florida, I called every one of them.

Every one of them I could find and tell them I was praying for them and that I cared about them and it was very hard to do. Every one of them said their child did not die in vain, that their wife or husband did not die in vain. So while it was difficult to do it was based on that.

Here is the lesson we should take from that which relates to the whole subject. Barack Obama became president and he abandoned Iraq. He left and when he left Al-Qaida was done for, Isis was created because of the void that we left, and that void now exists the caliphate the size of Indiana.

To honor the people who died we need to stop the Iran agreement for sure, because the Iranians have blood on their hands and we need to take out Isis with every tool."

"Governor Walker in February you said we needed to gain partners in the Arab world, which Arab nation not already in the US coalition has the potential to be our greatest partner?"

"Well I don't know about additional ones, we need to focus on the ones we already have. You look at Egypt probably the best relation we've had in Israel at least in my life time. Incredibly important, you look at the Saudi's leaders. I met with the Saudi leaders earlier this year. I asked them what's the greatest challenge in the world today set aside the Iran deal and they said the disengagement of America.

We are leading from behind under the Obama Clinton doctrine. America is a great country we need to stand up and start leading again, we'd have allies not just in Israel but throughout the Persian Gulf."

"Dr. Carson in one of his first acts as Commander in Chief President Obama signed an executive order banning enhanced interrogation techniques in war, as president would you bring back water-boarding?"

"Well thank you Megan I wasn't sure I was going to get to talk again."

Megan laughs as the crowd cheers his comment.

"What we do in order to get the information we need is our business and I wouldn't necessarily be broadcasting to everybody what we are going to do. We've gotten in to this mindset of fighting a political correct wars, there is no such thing as a political correct war.

The left will say that Carson doesn't believe in the Geneva Convention, Carson doesn't believe in fighting stupid wars. What we want to remember is that we want to utilize the tremendous intellect we have in the military to win wars.

I've talked to a lot of Generals and a lot of our advanced people and believe me if we gave them the mission which is what the Commander in Chief does, they would be able to carry it out and if we don't tie their hands behind their back they will do it effectively."

"The next series of questions is with Obama Care and the role of the Federal government. Mr. Trump Obama care is one of the things you call a disaster."

"A complete disaster." Trump comments.

"Saying it needs to be repealed and replaced."

"Correct."

"Now fifteen years ago you called yourself a liberal on health care. You were for a single care system a Canadian system. Why were you for it back then and why aren't you for it now?"

"First of all in July of 2004 I came out strongly against war with Iraq because it was going to destabilize the middle east and I'm the only one up here that knew that and had the vision to see it, and that is exactly what happened.

The middle east became totally destabilized, as far as a single payer, it works in Canada, it works in Scotland. It could of worked in a different age, which is the age you are talking about here. What I would like to see is a private system without the artificial lines around every State. I have a big company with thousands and thousands of employees and if I am negotiating in New York, or New Jersey, or California I have one bidder you know why? Because Insurance companies are making a fortune because they have control of the politicians, with the exception to the politicians on this stage.

They have total control of the politicians, they're making a fortune. Get rid of the artificial lines and you will have great plans. Then we have to take care of the people that can't take care of themselves and I will do that through a different system."

Interruption from Senator Paul.

"News flash the Republican parties been fighting against a single parent system for a decade. I think you are on the wrong side if you are still arguing for a single payer system."

Trump responds back to Senator Paul.

"I don't think you heard me, you're having a hard time tonight."

"Mr. Trump it's not just your past support for single payer health care, you've also supported a lot of other liberal policies, you've also donated to several Democratic candidates Hillary Clinton included, Nancy Pelosi. You've explained away those donations saying you did that to get business related favors and you said recently I quote. "When you give they do whatever the hell you want them to do."

Donald trump responds.

"You better believe it."

"So what specifically did they do?"

"If I ask them, if I need them, you know most of the people here on this stage I've given to you understand a lot of money."

Interruption from Mark Rubio. "Not me."

A few of the candidates laugh back and forth as they too state they received none from Donald Trump.

Mr. Trump responds. "I will tell you that are system is broken. I gave to many people before this before two months ago, because I am a business man, I give to everyone. When they call I give and when I need something from them two years later, three years later I call them, they are there for me, that's a broken system."

"What did you get from Hillary Clinton and Nancy Pelosi?"

"I'll tell you with Hillary Clinton I said be at my wedding and she came to my wedding and you know why? Because she had no choice because I gave to a foundation, a foundation that's suppose to do good. I didn't know her money would be used on private jets going all over the world, it was."

Mr. Walker interrupts. "Just a minute we spend a lot of time on Hillary Clinton and pitting us back and forth, let's be clear we should be talking about Hillary Clinton on that last subject, because everywhere Hillary Clinton touched is more messed up than it was before."

"Governor Huckabee, on Face Book John Pietricone. Asks this. "Will you abolish or take away the powers or cut the size of the EPA, IRS, and the Department of Education?"

"Now broadly the size of government is a big concern for Face Book users, Face Book persons and obviously conservatives as well. Year after year decade after decade there are promises to shrink government, but year after year decade after decade it doesn't happen, in fact it gets bigger even under Republican politicians. So the question is at this point is the government simply just too big for anyone person even a Republican to shrink?"

"It's not too big to shrink, but the problem is we have a Wall Street to Washington access of power that is controlled in political climate. The donor class feeds the political class who does the dance the donor class wants.

The result is the Federal government keeps getting bigger. Every governor on this stage will tell you the biggest fight they had was not the other party, it wasn't even the Legislature it was the Federal government who continued to put mandates on the States that we had to suck up and pay for and the fact is there is a lot of things happening at the Federal level that are absolutely beyond the jurisdiction of the Constitution.

This is power that should be shifted back to the States, whether it's the EPA, there is no role at the Federal level for the Department of Education and I am still the one that says we can get rid of the Internal Revenue Service if we pass the Fare tax, which is a tax on consumption rather than a tax on peoples income and move power back to where the founders believed it should have been all along."

"Dr. Carson do you agree with that?"

"Well I agree with, that we need a significantly new taxation system and the one that I have advocated is based on tithing, because I think God is a pretty fair guy. He said if you give me a tithe, it doesn't matter how much you make.

If you have a bumper crop you don't owe me triple tithes and if you had no crops at all you owe me no tithes. There must be something inherently fair about that and that's why I've advocated a proportionate tax system. You make 10 billion dollars you pay a billion dollars, you make 10 dollars you pay 1 dollar. Everybody gets treated the same way. You get rid of the deductions, you get rid of all the loopholes"

"Governor Busch you are one of the few people on the stage that advocates for common core education standards, reading and math. A lot of people on this stage vigorously oppose a Federal involvement in education. They say it should all be handled locally. President Obama's Secretary of Education, Arne Duncan has said most of the criticism of Common Core, is due to a fringe group of critics. Do you think that's accurate?"

"No I don't I don't believe the Federal government should be involved in the creations of standards directly or indirectly the creation of curriculum or content.

It is clearly a State responsibility. I am for higher standards, measure in an intellectual honest way with abundance school choice, ending social promotion and I know how to do this as governor of the State of Florida I created the first State wide voucher program in the country the second State wide voucher program in the country and the third State wide voucher program in the country.

We had rising student achievement across the board cause of high standards, robust accountability, ending social promotion in third grade, real school choice across the board, challenging the teacher's union and beating them is the way to go. Florida's low income kids had the greatest gains inside the country and graduation rates improved by fifty percent. That's what I am for."

"Senator Rubio why is Governor Busch wrong on the Common Core?"

"Well first of all I too believe in curriculum reform, it's very important in the 21st century. We do need curriculum reform and it should happen at State and local level. That is where educational level belongs, because if a parent is unhappy with what their child is being taught in school they can go to that local school board or that State Legislature, or their governor and get it changed.

Here is the problem with Common Core, the Department of Education like every Federal agency will never be satisfied.

They will not stop with it being a suggestion, they will turn it in to a mandate, in fact what they will begin to say to communities is you will not get Federal money unless you do things the way we want you to do it and they will use Common Core and any other requirements to use nationally to force it down the throats of the people of the States."

"Governor Busch do you agree with your old friend?"

"He is definitely my friend and I think the States ought to create these standards, if States want to opt out of Common Core fine. Just make sure your standards are high, because today in America a third of our kids after we spend more per student than any country in the world other than a couple surrounding areas to be honest with you. 30% are college and or career ready.

If we are going to compete in this world we are in today, there is no possible way we can do it by lowering expectations and dummying down everything. Children are going to suffer and families hearts are going to be broken that their kids won't be able to get a job in the 21st century.

We are half way through the first Republican debate, as we end this chapter and pick up the rest of the debate think about the questions and answers. Think about their speeches and their goals for this country. Think about if they are speaking to you as a politician who portrays themselves politically correct through the camera, or are they speaking as a true American who's ready and willing to lead.

CHAPTER SIX

As we head back to the second half of the first Republican presidential debate remember to listen to what the candidates are saying, but also look at what they have done, either in their political years or for those candidates that are new to politics what they have done in the private sector.

"Governor Kasich I'll start with you, Who ever that nominee is, whoever that Republican nominee is it looks like for now they will be facing off against Hillary Clinton. You know how she will come after you no matter who the Republican nominee is. She will say you support the rich while she supports the middle class, that you will want to suppress the women and minorities. She will say she wants to move the country forward while you the Republicans want to move the country back. If you are the nominee how will you answer that and take Hillary Clinton on?"

"I'll start off by my father being a mail man so I understand the folks all across this country, some of whom have trouble making ends meet, but I think she will come in a narrow way, the nominee of this party if they are going to win is going to have to come at it in a big way, which is pro growth, which is balancing budgets.

You know we were talking about this people were saying could we do it? I was the Chairman of the Budget Committee and the Lead architect the last time it happened in Washington and when we did it we had great economic growth, we cut taxes, and we had a big surplus. Economic growth is the key, it is the key to everything, but once you have economic growth it is important that we reach out to people that live in the shadows. To people that don't feel they get a fair deal. This includes people that are in the minority community, that includes people who feel they don't have a chance to move up.

America is a miracle country and we need to restore the since that the miracle will apply to you. Each and every one of the people in this country who is watching tonight, lift everybody, unite everybody, and build a stronger United States of America again. It will be and can be done."

His comment on America being a miracle country I disagree with, because it was no miracle we became a free nation, a strong powerful country. We became this through hard work and high morals and values. By showing respect to other countries while not letting them trample on our flag and our beliefs. Look at yesterday then look at today.

"Dr. Carson same question to you, if Hillary Clinton becomes the nominee and she comes at you with that kind of attack, how will you take her on?"

"If Hillary is the candidate which I doubt, that would be a dream come true. The fact of the matter is she is the epitome of the cycle progressive movement. She counts on the fact that people are uninformed. The Lewinski model, taking advantage of useful idiots, while I just happen to believe that people are not stupid. The way I will come at it is to educate people help people understand that it is that progressive movement that is causing them the problems.

You know you look at national debt and how it's being driven up. If I were trying to destroy this country I would try to create wedges and divide the people, drive the debt to an unsustainable level, then step off the stage as a world leader and let our enemies increase while we decrease our capacity as a military person and that is what she is doing."

Everything Dr. Ben Carson just said on destroying our country is everything I have been pointing out for the last couple years in my first two books of *Changing America with what if's*. with President Obama and Hillary Clinton.

"Governor Busch you had made a bold promise that you promised 4% economic growth and 19 million new jobs if you are fortunate enough to serve two terms as president. 19 million new jobs would be triple what your father and you brother did together and 4% growth the last president to reach that was Linden B. Johnson.

He did that during the height of the Vietnam war. The question, how on earth specifically would you pull that off?"

"We've done it 27 times since World War II. I think we need to lift our spirits and have high lofty expectations for this great country of ours. The 2% normal that the left is saying you can't do anything about is so dangerous for our country.

There are 6 million people living in poverty today, more than when Obama got elected 6 and a half million people working part time, most of whom want to work full time. We've created rules and taxes on top of every aspiration of people and the net result is we are not growing fast, incomes not growing. A 4% growth strategy means you fix a convoluted tax code you get in and change every aspiration of regulation that are job killers.

You get rid of Obama Care and replace it with something that doesn't suppress wages and kill jobs. You embrace the energy revolution in our country. Between this president and Hillary Clinton who can't even say she's for the Keystone XL Pipeline, even after she's left.

Give me a break. Of course we are for it we should be for these things to sustain high economic growth, and frankly fixing our immigration system and turning it in to an economic driver is part of this as well, we can do this."

"Governor Walker when you ran for governor of Wisconsin back in 2010, you promised you would create 250,000 new jobs in your first term, your first four years, in fact Wisconsin added barely half that and like 45th in the country in job growth. Now you are running for president and your promising an economic plan in which everyone will earn a piece of the American dream."

"Given your record in Wisconsin, why should voters believe you?"

"Well voters in Wisconsin elected me governor for the third time because they wanted someone that aimed high not low. Before I came in the unemployment rate was over 8% , it's now down to 4.6%. We more than made up for the jobs that were lost during the recession and the rate at what people are working is almost 5% higher than nationally.

People like Hilary Clinton think you grow the economy by growing Washington. One of the reports showed that last year that six of the top ten wealthiest counties in America were in or around Washington DC. I think most the people in America think the people, not Washington create jobs.

One of the best things we can do is get the government out of the way, repeal Obama Care, rein in all the auto control regulation, put in place all the above energy regulation policy, give all the people the education and skills they need to succeed and to lower the tax rate and reform the tax code. That's what I will do as president just like I did in Wisconsin."

You may want to look at those jobs he did create. Were they all full time or part time? Were they minimum wage or were they higher wage an hour jobs? Were they jobs with benefits? What about whether or not the seasonal jobs were included into the whole array of statistics?

"Governor Christie I am going to engage you and Governor Huckabee in a subject that is a big issue in both of your campaigns, and that is entitlement reform. You say to save the system you want to raise the retirement age and to cut benefits for social security and Medicare. You say some of the candidates on the stage are lying. Governor Huckabee says he can save social security and Medicare without doing any of that. Is he lying?"

"No he's not lying, he's just wrong, there is a difference. I am the only guy on this stage that has put out a detailed 12 point plan on entitlement reform and here is why. Because 71% of federal spending right now is on entitlements and debt service, 71% and we have spent the last hour and five minutes talking about the other 29% and no time on the 71% and that makes no sense. Now let me tell you exactly what we would do on social security. We would raise the retirement 2 years and phase in over 25 years that mean we raise it 1 month a year for 25 years when we are all living longer and living better lives.

Secondly we would have means for social security for those that are making over 200,000 dollars a year in retirement income, and have 4 to 5 million dollars in liquid assets saved.

They don't need that social security check. Social security is meant to be, that no one has worked harder and played by the rules and paid in to the system grows old in poverty in America if we don't deal with this problem it will bankrupt our country, it will lead to massive tax increases, neither one we want in this country."

"Governor Huckabee, you say changing entitlements, the kind of things Governor Christie is talking about will be breaking a promise to the American people. You say you can keep those programs, save social security save Medicare without those reforms through a fair tax which is a broad tax on consumption. Please explain to Governor Christie how that would work and how you could save these programs without the kind of painful reforms he says we need."

"Let's all be reminded 60 million Americans are on social security, 60 million. A third of those people depend on 90% of their income from social security. Nobody in this country is on social security because they made the decision when they were starting work at 14 that they wanted to entrust some of their money with the government. The government took it out of their checks whether they wanted them to or not.

If a person goes to 65 they are going to go 51 years with the government reaching in to their pocket every paycheck, now here is the point. Whose fault is it, if the system is screwed up? Is it the recipients or is it the government?

If congress wants to mess with the retirement program, why don't we have them start by changing their retirement program and not have one, instead of talking about getting rid of social security and Medicare that was robbed 700 billion dollars to pay for Obama Care. It always is the government figures it can do this off the backs of people, many of them are poor and depend on that money and I think that's just fundamentally lying to the people and stealing from them and we shouldn't be doing it."

Governor Christie responds.

"Now I don't disagree with Congress's retirement program. I'm a governor I don't have a retirement program in my State and I don't disagree with that, but here's the news for the American people. He is complaining about the lying and stealing, the lying and stealing has already occurred, the trust fund is filled with IOU's. We can't just fix the problem by Congress retirement, it's worth about this much."

Governor Christie holds up to fingers displaying a minute amount.

"We need to go with the fundamental problem, and the fundamental problem is this system is broken, it has been stolen from we have been lied to. We need a strong leader to tell the truth and fix it."

"You ask about how we fund it, one of the reasons social security is in so much trouble is because the only funding stream is by the people that get a wage. The people getting wages is declining dramatically.

Most of the income in this country is made by people at the top who get dividends and capital gains. The fair tax transforms the process in which we fund social security and Medicare because the money paid at consumption is paid by everybody, including illegal's, prostitutes, pimps, drug dealers, all the people who are freeloading off the system now. That is why it ought to be a transformed system."

"Mr. Trump you have talked a lot about you are the person on this stage to grow the economy. I want to ask you about your business record. Trump Corporations, Trump Corporations, casinos and hotels have declared bankruptcy 4 times over the last quarter century. In 2011 you told Forbes Magazine that I use the laws of the country to my advantage, but at the same time financial experts involved in those bankruptcies say that lenders to those companies lost billions of dollars.

Question sir with that record why should we trust you to run the nations business?

"Because I have used the laws of this country, just like the greatest people that you read about every day in business have used the laws of this country the chapter laws to do a great job for my company, for myself, for my employees, for my family etc.

I have never gone bankrupt by the way, I have never. Out of hundreds of my deals. On four occasions I have taken advantage of the laws of this country, like other people.

I'm not going to name names because I'm not going to embarrass them, but virtually every person that you read about on the front page of the business sections they've used the law.

The difference is that when somebody else uses those laws nobody writes about it. When I use it they say Trump, Trump, Trump. The fact is I built a net worth of over 10 billion dollars. I have a great, great company. I employ thousands of people and I am very proud of the job I've done, again Chris hundreds and hundreds of deals four times I've taken advantage of the laws and frankly so has everybody else in my position."

"Well sir let's just talk about the latest example, which is Trump Entertainment Resorts, which went bankrupt in 2009. In that case a lone lenders to your company lost over a billion dollars and over 1100 people were laid off."

"Well I laid off, let me tell you about the lenders. First of all these lenders aren't babies, they are total killers. These are not the nice sweet little people you think ok. You know you are living in a world of make believe Chris, if you want to know the truth and I had the good sense to leave Atlantic City which by the way a Ceasers just went bankrupt, every company Chris can tell you. Every company virtually in Atlantic City went bankrupt.

Let me just tell you, I had the good sense and I've gotten a lot of credit in the financial pages. Seven years ago I left Atlantic City before it totally cratered. I've made a lot of money in Atlantic City and I am very proud of it, I wanted to tell you that.

Very, very proud of that, by the way this country right now owes 19 trillion dollars and they need somebody like me to straighten out that mess."

"Senator Rubio more than 3,000 people sent us questions about the economy and jobs on Face Book and here is a question from Tania Cioloko."

"Please describe one action you would do to make the economic environment more favorable for small businesses and entrepreneurs and anyone dreaming of opening up their own business?"

"That is a great question. First of all it starts with leaders that can recognize the economy we live in today is dramatically different than the one we lived in 5 years ago. It's an economy that has now pushed us into global competition with dozens of countries around the world.

Now the big companies that have connection with Washington, they can affect policies to help them but the small companies like Tania is talking about are the ones that are struggling.

The first thing we need to do is even out the tax code for businesses so that we lower their tax rate to 25% just like we need to lower it for all businesses. We need to have a regulatory budget in America that limits the amount of regulations on our economy. We need to repeal and replace Obama Care and we need to improve higher education so that people can have access to the skills they need for 21st century jobs and last but not least we need to repeal Dodd Frank it is eviscerating small businesses and small banks.

Over 40% of small and mid size banks that loan money to small businesses have been wiped out since Dodd Franks has passed. We need to repeal or replace Dodd Frank. We need to make America fair again for all businesses, but especially those that are being run by small business owners."

"Yesterday gentleman, President Obama criticized Republican law makers trying to block the Iran deal, calling them a name, adding hard liners in Iran chanting death to America were quote making common cause with the Republican caucus. Here is what two of your opponents on the earlier debate stage said about Obama.

"I will tell you one thing I would rather have Carly Fiorina over there doing our negotiations then John Kerry, maybe we would have gotten a deal where we didn't give everything away. The issue for us is to have a Congress stand up and not just say no, but hell no to this money going to a regime." Spoken be Rick Perry.

"When America does not lead the world is a dangerous and tragic place. This is a bad deal, Obama broke every rule with negotiation, yes our allies are not perfect, but Iran is at the heart of most of the evil going on in the middle east and their proxy."

"First I want to ask a couple of you this. First Governor Walker. You said you would tear up the Iran deal on day one. If this deal is undone what then?"

"Well first off I still remember as a kid tying a yellow ribbon around the tree in front of my house during the 444 days that Iran held 52 Americans hostage. Iran is not a place we should be doing business with. To me you terminate the deal on day one. You reinstate the sanctions authorized by Congress. You go to congress and put in place even more crippling sanctions and convince our allies to do the same.

This is not just bad with Iran, it's bad with Isis it's tide together and once and for all we need a leader who is going to stand up and do something about it. It is yet another example of failed foreign policy of the Obama Clinton doctrine."

"Senator Paul would you tear up the deal day one?"

"I oppose the Iranian deal and would vote against it. I don't think the president negotiated from a position of strength, but I don't immediately discount negotiations. I am a Reagan conservative. Reagan did negotiate with the Soviets, but you have to negotiate from a position of strength. I think President Obama gave away to much too early. If you are going to have negotiations you must believe the Iranians are going to somehow comply. I asked this question to John Kerry, do you believe they are trustworthy? And he said no. So I said how are we going to get them to comply. I would have never released the sanctions before there was consistent evidence of compliance."

"Governor Huckabee what do you think of what Senator Paul just said?"

"Ronald Reagan said trust but verify, President Obama is trust but vilify. He trusts our enemies and vilifies anyone who disagrees with him and the reason we disagree with him has nothing to do with party and everything to do with the incredible dangerous place this place is going to be in a result of a deal in which we got nothing. We didn't even get 4 hostages out, we get nothing and Iran gets everything they want.

We said we would have any where any time negotiations and inspections, we gave that up. We said we would make sure they didn't have any nuclear capacity, we gave that up.

The president can't tell us what we got, I can tell you what the world got. The world got a margining nuclear power, that didn't as the soviets say we might defend ourselves in time of war, what the Iranians have said is we will wipe Israel off the face of the map and we will bring death to America. When someone points a gun at your head by God you ought to take them seriously and we need to take that seriously."

"We are going to start now with some social issues, Governor Busch let's start with you. Many Republicans have been outraged by a series of videos on planned parenthood. You now say you support ending this funding this organization, however in late 2014 right before you started your campaign you sat on a board the Bloomberg charity that publically gave tens of millions of dollars to Planned Parenthood while you were a director.

How could you not know about these well publicized donations and if you did know how can you openly help a charity committed to abortion rights?

"I joined the Bloomberg foundation because Mike Bloomberg's shared meaningful education reform, that is why I was on it we never had a debate about the budget. It was presented and we approved it, not item by item. Here is what my record as Governor of the State of Florida. I defunded Planned Parenthood. I created a culture of life in our State. We were the only State to appropriate money for a Crisis Pregnancy Centers, we expanded dramatically the number of adoptions out of our foster care system. We created, we did parental notification laws.

We ended partial birth abortions, we did all of this and we were the first State to do chose life license plates, now 29 States have done it and tens of millions of dollars have gone to create a culture where more people, more babies are adopted."

It is interesting that he said he didn't know and he didn't check it item by item. This is the guy they called Veto Corlioni, who vetoed 2,500 separate line items.

"Did you know?"

"No I didn't know, it doesn't matter I was working on this board because of education. My record is clear. My record is a pro life governor is not in dispute.

I am completely pro life and I believe we should have a culture of life, it is affirmed by my culture of faith from beginning to end and I did this not because it related to unborn babies, I did it at the end of life issues as well. This is something that goes way beyond politics. I hope we one day get to the point where we respect life and its fullest form across the board."

"Senator Rubio, you favor a rape and incest exception to abortion band, Cardinal Timothy Dolan of New York said those bands are preposterous. He said they discriminate against an entire race of human beings. If you believe that life begins at conception which you say you do, how do you justify ending a life just because it starts violently through no fault of the baby?"

"Megan, first of all I'm not sure that is a correct assessment of my record, I would go on to add."

Megan interrupts him. "You don't favor a rape and an incest exemption?"

"No and I never said that and never advocated that. What I have advocated is that we pass law in this country that all humane life at every stage of its humane development is worthy of protection, matter of fact I think that law already exists. It's called the Constitution of the United States. Let me go further I believe every single person is entitled to protection of the laws whether they can vote or not, whether they can speak or not, whether they can hire a lawyer or not, whether they have a birth certificate or not.

I think future generations will look back at this history of our country and call us barbarians for murdering millions of babies that we never gave them a chance to live."

"Mr. Trump you said in 1999 you were very pro choice even supporting partial birth abortion, you favored a weapon assault band as well. In 2004 you said you mostly identified as a Democrat, even in this campaign many of your candidates say you even sound more like a Democrat then a Republican calling several of your candidates clowns and puppets. When did you actually become a Republican?"

Donald Trump smiles and shrugs his shoulders.

"I don't think they like me very much." As he points toward the mediators.

"I'll tell you what I have evolved over many issues over the years and you know who else has Ronald Reagan on many issues. I am pro life. If you look at the question I was in business they asked me a question to pro life or choice and I said if you let it run I hate the concept of abortion and since then have very much evolved.

What happened was a friend of mine was going to have a child and it was going to be aborted and it wasn't aborted and that child today is a total superstar. He is a great, great guy and I saw that and other instances and I am very proud to say that I am pro life.

As far as being a Republican I come from a place that is almost exclusively Democrat and I have really started to see some of the negatives as an example I have a lot of liking for this man, but the last couple of months under his brothers (referring to Jeb Busch's brother)administration were a catastrophe and unfortunately those few months gave us President Obama and you can't be happy about that."

There is 30 minutes left of the first debate if you want to watch it on you tube it is available. Just to give you a current update today is Oct 1st 2015 It also happens to be my twins birthday, they turned 14 years old today. Their future depends on our decisions that we make. It is vital that for those that Love this country and wish to live their lives and watch their children grow and live successfully, that we need to make sure we cross our T's and dot our I's.

Currently two of the candidates have already dropped out Governor Perry and Governor Walker. You may ask why does this matter, it matters because we could go back to their speeches and see how dedicated they were and how committed, yet they have just thrown in the towel.

I understand it takes money to run and compete, which should tell us right there that someone with no money could never be President. There are more debates a head of us as we continue our journey to the next President. Let's look at our past presidents from Washington to Obama.

American pride, American Respect

Let the next explosion be the sound of clapping
hands as we congratulate our next president.

America is the land of the free but freedom comes
with a price, peace through power can save our
enemy the thought of what if, by knowing we will.

The
United States of America
Is
Back

CHAPTER SEVEN

This chapter covers all the presidents from before, starting in order, all the way to our current president. I will not cover everything but I will give you a bit of information on each one. When we are done you will have a different outlook on the presidents, or again maybe not. The following information came from https://en.wikipedia.org/wiki/List_of_Presidents_of_the_United_States

History shows change throughout the years, it shows patterns in certain situations and or people. This is the time to sit down read and put your mind to work as you gather all this information as we seek a future president to lead our great nation.

Again we have to look at yesterday knowing we didn't know then what we know now. If you are ready we will get ready to head way back before my time and yours, before TV and XBOX. We are here now because of the generations before us Do we not owe it to our children's generations and their children?

George Washington: was born in 1732 and died in 1799. He was from the State of Virginia. His term in office was from April 30, 1789 – March 4, 1797. He served two terms in office and was associated with the Independent Party. His Vice President was John Adams.

George Washington was the first President of the United States of America. He was the Commander in Chief of the Continental Army during the Revolutionary War. He presided over the convention that drafted the current United States Constitution.

He came from a wealthy family that owned tobacco plantations and slaves in which he inherited. He owned hundreds of slaves though out his life time. Washington's incumbency has left a few things that are still in use today, such as the cabinet system, inaugural address, along with the title Mr. President.

He supported Alexander Hamilton's programs to satisfy all debt, both Federal and State. He remained nonpartisan never joining the Federalist party, but did support much of their policies. President George Washington has monuments made of him and is on our currency that we use every day. He was one of the Founding Fathers of the United States of America. He was an officer in the military and was a battle tested leader who fought hard for America.

The 1st President of the United States of America

John Adams: He was born in 1735 and died in 1799. He was from the State of Massachusetts. John Adams served one term in office as President of the United States from March 4, 1797 to March 4, 1801 He was associated with the Federalist Party. His Vice President was Thomas Jefferson.

John Adams was a lawyer, author, statesman along with being a diplomat. He was one of the Founding Fathers. He promoted Republicanism and a strong government. He served two terms himself as the Vice President for George Washington. He assisted Thomas Jefferson in drafting the Declaration of Independence.

John Adams encountered fierce criticism from both the Jefferson's Republicans, along with his own Federalist Party. He also signed the Alien and Sedition Act, which were four bills passed into law during the undeclared war with France also known as the Quasi War.

At age 16 Adams entered Harvard College and obtained a bachelor of arts degree. John Adams opposed the Stamp Act of 1765, which the British Parliament imposed without consulting the American legislature on collecting payments of direct tax on colonies stamped documents.

He was counsel for British soldiers who were charged with killing five civilians in the Boston Massacre. He argued on Blackstone's Ratio, which was better to let ten guilty go than to make one innocent suffer.

The 2nd President of the United States of America

Thomas Jefferson: Was born in 1743 and died in 1826. He was from the State of Virginia. Thomas Jefferson served two terms as the President of the United State from March 4, 1801 to March 4, 1809. He was associated with the Democratic Republican Party. He previously held the office of Vice President for President John Adams.

Thomas Jefferson was one of the Founding Fathers and the principle author of the Declaration of Independence He was a passionate and enthusiastic supporter of the principles of Republicanism and the rights of the individual. In 1785 he became the United States Minister to France, and later the First United States Secretary of State.

The Republican administration actually reduced the military after peace negations with France after the election in 1800. Thomas Jefferson purchased a large mass of the Louisiana Territory from Napoleonic France, this is when he sent out the Lewis and Clark Expedition. Three years later he initiated a short campaign against the Barbary Coast States in North Africa, defending American shipping.

Jefferson's earliest memory is of him being handed to a slave on horseback and carried away fifty miles on horseback to their new home. Thomas Jefferson and his brother divided the Jefferson estate He received approximately 5,000 acres and between 20 and 40 slaves.

The 3rd President of the United States of America

James Madison: was born in 1751 and died in 1836 He was from the State of Virginia. He served two terms in office as the President of the United States from March 4, 1809 till March 4, 1817. He was associated with the Democratic Republican Party, he also never held the office of Vice President, but held the office of Secretary of State from 1801 till 1809.

The Vice President office was vacant from April 20, 1812 till March 4, 1813 during his term as President. It again became vacant on March 4, 1817. James Madison was an American Statesman and Theorist. He is hailed as the Father of the Constitution in regards to the drafting of the Constitution as well as an author of the Bill of rights. He spent most of his adult life as a politician.

As Secretary of State he supervised the Louisiana Purchase, doubling our country's size. He led our Country in the War of 1812. He too was a slave holder, he inherited his plantation known as Montpelier. He owned hundreds of slaves throughout his lifetime. They were used to harvest the tobacco and other crops. Madison supported the Three Fifths Compromise which allowed three fifth of the enumerated population of slaves to be counted for representation. James Madison grew up the oldest of twelve kids, once again it was common back then to have large families.

In 1775 he was commissioned as a Colonel in the Orange County Militia. He never served in combat due to poor health.

The 4ᵗʰ President of the United States of America

James Monroe: was born in 1758 and died in 1831. He too was from the State of Virginia. He served two terms in office as the President of the United States from March 4, 1817 till March 4, 1825. He was associated with the Democratic Republican Party. He held the office of Secretary of State from 1811 till 1817, at which time he took over as President of the United States.

James Monroe was the last of the Founding Fathers of the United States. He was the last president from the Virginia Dynasty and of the Republican generation. James Monroe fought in the Revolutionary War and was wounded, hit by a musket ball in the shoulder during the Battle of Trenton.

He served as a delegate in the Continental Congress as an anti Federalist to the Virginia convention that considered ratification to the United States Constitution. He opposed it stating it gave too much power to the government. He was the last president of the first party system. He also bought Florida from Spain. The Treaty of 1819 secured the border of the United States along the 42nd parallel to the Pacific Ocean, this with the Treaty of 1818 extended from the Atlantic to the Pacific helping to build an American global empire.

James Monroe sold his small plantation to enter law and politics ,but later fulfilled his dreams by owning a large plantation. He was hardly ever there and his slaves were treated harshly. He incurred debt by living lavishly and sold property and slaves to pay off debts.

The 5th President of the United States of America

John Quincy Adams: was born in 1767 and died in 1848. He was from the State of Massachusetts. He served one term in office from March 4, 1825 till March 4, 1829. He was associated with the Democratic Republican Party. He served as Secretary of State from 1817 till 1825, at which time he was elected President of the United States.

He is the Son to the Second President of the United States, John Adams. He is the first president of a select few who would follow their family's legacy into the White House. John Quincy Adams played an important role in negotiating in the Treaty of Ghent, which ended the War of 1812. He negotiated with Britain over the United States Northern border with Canada and negotiated with Spain the Annexation of Florida. Historians see him as one of the greatest diplomats and Secretary's of State in American history.

John Quincy Adams growing disgust for slavery made him a leading opponent of the slave power. He believed that if a Civil War broke out that the president could abolish slavery. It appears that of all the presidents we have covered so far only President John Adams and his Son John Quincy Adams never owned slaves.

This is important to know as we cover the presidents and the time in which they served. It goes to show you that not everyone back then was for slavery that there were people that sided for the African Americans and their communities.

The 6th President of the United States of America

Andrew Jackson: was born in 1767 and died in 1845. He was from the State of Tennessee. He served two terms as the President of the United States from March 4, 1829 till March 4, 1837. He was associated with the Democratic Party. He previously held the office of U.S. Senator of Tennessee.

There was a vacancy in the Vice Presidency from December 28, 1832 till March 4, 1833, at which time Martin Van Buren held office during Andrew Jackson's second term from March 4, 1833 till March 4, 1837. He was elected in the House of Representatives and then to the Senate. He was appointed Colonel in the Tennessee Militia in 1801. His family supported the Revolutionary cause and he was a courier. He was captured at age 13 and mistreated by his captors.

Andrew Jackson owned hundreds of slaves that worked on the Hermitage Plantation, in which he acquired in 1804. Jackson gained fame during the War of 1812 where he gained a victory over the British at the Battle of New Orleans. He also killed a man in a dual over honor in regards to his wife.

Jackson's supporters founded what became the Democratic Party. As President he was aware of a threat of secession from South Carolina over the Tariff of Abominations.

The 7ᵗʰ President of the United States of America

Martin Van Buren: was born in 1782 and died in 1862. He was from the State of New York. He served one term as the President of the United States from March 4, 1837 till March 4, 1841. He was associated with the Democratic Party. He previously held the office of Vice President and was Secretary of State both under President Jackson. His Vice President was Richard Mentor Johnson.

President Van Buren inability to deal with the economic chaos, known as the Panic of 1837 lead to his defeat in the 1840 election. He was blamed for the depression that took place. He tried to keep control of Federal Funds in an independent Treasury and not in State Banks.

He was most known for being a political organizer who built the modern Democratic Party in the new second party system. He was a major supporter for President Jackson earlier who had then made him Secretary of State, but as President he struggled to accomplish much.

As we go through the presidents it will be interesting to see under which party that we struggle economically the most and under which party our military becomes weak. It may not be the Party's fault but the leaders themselves or a combination of the two.

President Van Buren's father was a farmer and owned the Kinder Hook Inn, along with six slaves.

The 8th President of the United States of America

William Henry Harrison: was born in 1773 and died in 1841. He was from the State of Ohio. He was elected President of the United States from March 4, 1841 till April 4, 1841, where he died of pneumonia. He was associated with the Whig Party. He held the presidency the shortest term due to dying one month later.

He held the office of Minister to Columbia prior to his presidency from 1828 till 1829. John Tyler was his Vice President. He was an American military officer and the last president born as a British subject.

He gained national fame when he led U.S. forces against the American Indians, where he earned the nickname Tippecanoe. He was a General in the War of 1812. And the oldest President to ever held office up until Ronald Reagan.

William Henry Harrison was supposedly influenced by anti slavery Quakers and Methodists at the academy in Southampton county.

Governor Henry Lee, a friend of William's father persuaded him to join the army and within 24 hours of meeting with him was commissioned to ensign in the U.S. Army 1st Infantry Regiment.

The 9th President of the United States of America

John Tyler: was born in 1790 and died in 1862. He was from the State of Virginia and was president from April 4, 1841 to March 4, 1845, one month short of a full term He was associated with the Whig Party from April 4, 1841 till September 13, 1841, at which time he then associated himself with the Independent Party through the end of his presidency.

He held the previous office of Vice President at which time he took over as President due to the sudden death of President William Henry Harrison. The Vice President office became vacant and remained vacant throughout his term as President. He was the first president to take office without being elected into office.

He was known as a supporter of State's rights. He was willing to support nationalists policies as long as they didn't infringe on the State's rights. He sought to strengthen and preserve the Union through territory expansion. He was the first president to switch parties during his presidency.

He came from an aristocratic Virginia family. His precedence would then govern future successions and become the twenty fifth Amendment. He found much of the Whig platform unconstitutional and vetoed several of its party's bills. He was the first president to have one of his veto's overturned by Congress.

The 10th President of the United States of America

James K. Polk: was born in 1795 and died in 1849. He was from the State of Tennessee and served one term as President of the United States from March 4, 1845 till March 4 1849. He was associated with the Democratic Party and held the office of Governor of Tennessee prior to his term as President. His Vice President was George M. Dallas.

He was born in Mecklenburg County North Carolina, but lived and represented Tennessee. He was the 17th Speaker of the House of Representatives. He defeated Henry Clay of the Whig Party by promising to annex Texas.

He over saw the opening of the Naval Academy and the Smithsonian Institute. He died three months after his Presidential term ended of Cholera.

His father was a slave holder and successful farmer. When James was taken as a child to church to be baptized his father refused to declare his belief in Christianity and was then not baptized. In 1822 Polk joined the Militia and was a Captain in the Calvary Regiment of the 5th Brigade.

Polk was given the nickname Napoleon of the Stump for his oratory.

The 11th President of the United States of America

Zachary Taylor: was born in 1784 and died in 1850. He was from the State of Louisiana He was elected President of the United States and served from March 4, 1849 till July 9, 1850 when he died cutting him short of his term in office. His Vice President Millard Fillmore took over the duties of President, leaving the Vice presidency vacant

Zachary Taylor was a Major General in the U.S. Army 1st.Infantry Regiment. He was a career officer in the military . Prior to him becoming President. He was also associated with the Whig Party. His status as a national hero as a result of their victories in the Mexican American war help him get elected into office.

He grew up in a prominent family of planters who migrated from Virginia to Kentucky. He was commissioned as an officer in 1808 and made a name for himself as a Captain in the War of 1812. His nickname was *Old Rough and Ready*.

Taylor didn't push for the expansion of slavery even though he was a Southern slaveholder himself. He urged settlers in New Mexico and California to bypass the territorial stage and draft constitutions for Statehood setting the stage for the Compromise of 1850. Zachary Taylor died suddenly from a stomach related illness.

The 12th President of the United States of America

Millard Fillmore: was born in 1800 and died in 1874. He was from the State of New York. He became president on July 9, 1850 when President Zachary Taylor died while still in office. He was the second President that entered through the Vice presidency, rather than by election. He served one term from July 9, 1850 till March 4, 1853.He was associated with the Whig Party.

He was also the last president not to be associated with either the Republican or Democratic Parties. President Fillmore was the only Whig President to not die in office or get expelled from office. He was a lawyer and served as a U.S. Representative in the State Legislature.

As an anti slavery moderate he was against abolitionists demands on excluding slavery from all the territory gained in the Mexican War, but rather supported the Compromise of 1850 which briefly ended the crisis.

Fillmore was a member of the New York Militia and gained the rank of Major, he served as Inspector of New York's 47th Brigade. The University of Buffalo which is still operational he helped fund.

When Fillmore took office his entire Cabinet turned over as the current administration all resigned. He appointed persons who all but one, were in favor of the Compromise of 1850.

The 13th President of the United States of America

Franklin Pierce: was born in 1804 till 1869. He was from the State of New Hampshire. He served one term as President of the United States from March 4, 1853 till March 4, 1857. He was associated with the Democratic Party.

He served prior to the presidency as a Brigadier General in the U.S. Army. He was a Northern Democrat who saw the Abolitionists movement as a threat to the unity of the Nation. He was responsible for the Kansas-Nebraska Act along with the Fugitive slave Act. These were laws that were passed to see that slaves were returned to their owners or State from where they came. He served in both the House of Representatives and the Senate.

He took part in the Mexican American War as a Brigadier General. His popularity dropped in the North after he supported the Kansas Nebraska Act which nullified the Missouri Compromise. His reputation suffered further during the Civil War where he made it public he was against Abraham Lincoln.

According to historians and political commentators President Franklin Pierce was ranked one of the worst presidents, but I am sure there is a president that is going to change that once we get to him.

The 14ᵗʰ President of the United States if America

James Buchanan: was born in 1791 and died in 1868. He was from the State of Pennsylvania. He served one term as President of the United States from March 4, 1857 till March 4, 1861. He was associated with the Democratic Party. He held the office prior to President, as the Minister to the United Kingdom. John C. Breckenridge was his Vice President.

He served immediately after the Civil War as President. He served in the United States House of Representatives, representing Pennsylvania. He also served as Minister to Russia and was the last former Secretary of State to serve as president.

He was known as a Northerner with Southern sympathies. Buchanan tried to create peace between the North and the South, but instead alienated both sides to where the South declared their secession in what became the Civil War.

Historians have also labeled him one of the worst presidents, due to his lack to identify a grounds for peace, or the division between both pro and anti slavery. He is the last president born in the 18th century and was the only president to be a lifelong bachelor.

The 15th President of the United States of America

CHAPTER EIGHT

We have just covered the first 15 presidents along with 72 years of history. How many of these presidents came from wealth of money and land, power over people, slaves and servants? How many served their country to make it better for us rather than for just them or their chosen few? How many different political parties have we seen in these 72 years? How much influence did these parties have on our presidents?

We are getting ready to look at the next fifteen presidents, what we find out about them will either continue our beliefs that there are no differences in our presidents, or maybe that our presidents change with the times as do we. Have we noticed how many presidents studied law and exactly how many years did it take them to get a degree? What about military experience when we look at our presidents, after all he is the Commander in Chief in time of war. If you are ready let's get back to our past presidents as we move forwards in time getting ever closer to the present.

Abraham Lincoln was born in 1809 and died in 1865 He was from the State of Illinois He served one complete term as President of the United States from March 4, 1861 till April 15, 1865 where he died by assassination in his second term in office. He was associated with the Republican and the Republican national union. His previous office that he held was that of U.S. Representative of Illinois.

He had two different Vice Presidents during his term in office starting with, Hannibal Hamlin March 4, 1861 till March 4, 1865 then Andrew Johnson from March 4, 1865 till April 15, 1865, at which time Johnson took over as President.

Lincoln led the United States through the Civil War, the bloodiest of battles. He preserved the Union and abolished slavery, strengthened the Federal government and modernized the economy. He was largely self educated and became a lawyer in Illinois, but grew up in Kentucky. He became a leader in the new Republican Party that was the majority in the State of Illinois in 1858.

His victory to the presidency led seven Southern States to form the Confederate States of America, which then led to the Civil War. Abraham Lincoln is known also for his Gettysburg Address. It endorsed the principles of Nationalism, Republicanism, Equal Rights, Democracy and Liberty. Lincolns goal was to reunite the nation. He has been viewed as one of the best presidents ever.

The 16th President of the United States of America

Andrew Johnson: was born in 1808 and died in 1875. He was from the State of Tennessee. He served one term in office from April 15, 1865 till March 4, 1869. He was associated with the Democratic, National Union and Independent Parties. He served as Vice President prior to him taking over as President of the United States due to President Lincoln being assassinated.

The President favored quick restoration of the seceded States to join the Union. He battled with Congress which was mostly Republican. The house of Representatives tried to impeach him. He was the first President to be impeached but he was acquitted in the Senate by one vote.

Johnson was born into poverty, but never let that stop him as he became an alderman and a mayor. He then went on to the Tennessee House of Representatives served in the Senate and again moved further into politics and became Governor of Tennessee all the way up to President.

Johnson opposed the 14th Amendment which gave citizenship to former slaves He is seen as one of the worst presidents due to his opposition to Federally guaranteed rights for African Americans.

If we were to think of this president in our time we would all dislike him for thinking of the African American as less than human. Today we are all about equal and beyond.

The 17th President of the United States of America

Ulysses S. Grant: was born in 1822 and died in 1885. He was from the State of Illinois. He served two terms in office as the President of the United States from March 4, 1869 till March 4, 1877. He was associated with the Republican Party, prior to that he served as Commanding General of the U.S. Army from 1864 to 1869.

As President he had two different Vice Presidents, Schuyler Colfax from March 4, 1869 till March 4, 1873, and Henry Wilson from March 4, 1873 till November 22, 1875. After that the office of Vice President lay vacant to the end of Grant's term.

As Commanding General he worked closely with President Lincoln as he led the Union Army to victory over the Confederacy during the Civil War. He was a West Point graduate. He led the Republicans against the Confederate Nationalism and slavery. He incorporated displaced slaves into the Union War effort. In his second term he was credited with leading the nation in a severe economic depression.

Grant was known for his ability to work with and ride the most challenging of horses and was sometimes injured.

During his presidency he prosecuted the Ku Klux Klan and enforced civil and voting rights using the Army and Department of Justice.

The 18ᵗʰ President of the United States of America

Rutherford B. Hayes: was born in 1822 and died in 1893. He was from the State of Ohio. He served one term as President of the United States from March 4, 1877 to March 4, 1881. He was associated with the Republican party. Prior to Rutherford B. Hayes becoming president he served as U.S. Representative of Ohio from 1863 to 1881.

During the Civil War he left his political career and joined the Union Army, he was recognized for his bravery and promoted to Major General. He was wounded five times, most seriously at the Battle of South Mountain. After the war he served in Congress as a Republican. He served three terms as Governor of Ohio.

As president he over saw the end of the Reconstruction. In 1876 he lost the popular vote to Samuel J Tilden, while winning the highly scrutinized electoral college vote. It created the Compromise of 1877, it was an unwritten deal that settled the dispute of the election and pulled Federal troops out of politics.

Hayes believed in equal treatment regardless of race. He also believed in improvement through education. The Dawes Act of 1887 adopted by Congress saw to it that Indians that lived separate from their tribes and took these lots that had been surveyed would be allowed citizenship.

The 19th President of the United States of America

James A. Garfield: was born in 1831 and died in 1881. He was from the State of Ohio. He served six months of a four year term as President of the United States. His term ended shortly after office as he died only months later. He was associated with the Republican Party and prior to his presidency was the U.S. Representative from Ohio.

President James A. Garfield was assassinated cutting his presidency short. He did nine terms in the House of Representatives and is the only sitting House member to be elected President.

He was raised on an Ohio farm by his widowed mother. He went to college at Williams College in Williamstown Massachusetts, after graduating there went a year later into politics He was against the Confederate Secession.

His accomplishments while in office included a resurgence of presidential authority against senatorial courtesy in executive appointments, energizing American Naval power and purging corruption in the Post office. Garfield knew his place was in the Union Army during the war but per the request of Governor William Dennison, he aborted his military ambition and remained in the Legislature. The only battle that Garfield personally commanded was the Battle at Middle Creek.

The 20ᵗʰ President of the United States of America

Chester A. Arthur: was born in 1829 and died in 1886. He was from the State of New York. He served one term as President of the United States from September 19, 1881 till March 4, 1885. He was associated with the Republican Party. Prior to his presidency he was Vice President of the United States. Due to the assassination of President Garfield he moved right in to the position of President without having to be elected.

During his Presidential stay the Vice President positioned remained vacant till the next election. The Pendleton Civil Service Reform Act was a major focal point in his administration, it became Federal law in 1883 establishing that government jobs should be awarded on the basis of merit instead of by political association. Today Illinois uses a similar test called the Ethics test which is used to show or present a person's ethical stand on certain issues and supervisors can then say he had been told, taught, or informed taking the responsibility away from them as any typical politician would do.

Arthur practiced law in New York, he was quartermaster General in the New York Militia during the Civil War. Alexander McClure an author later wrote no man had ever entered the office of President so distrusted and retired so respected by both friend and foe. These are the type presidents that truly make a difference, when even their adversaries respect them.

The 21st President of the United States of America

Grover Cleveland: was born in 1837 and died in 1908. He was from the State of New York. He served two terms in office as President of the United States, but serving only one term at a time from March 4, 1885 till March 4 1889 and then having been reelected served the second term from March 4, 1893 till March 4, 1897, being the first President and only president to ever get re elected in such a manner. He was associated with the Democratic Party. Prior to his presidency he was Governor of New York.

He was the winner of the popular vote for president three times in the years, 1884, 1888, and 1892. Grover Cleveland alongside Woodrow Wilson were two democrats that would be elected as Democratic presidents in a Republican dominated era.

In his second term in office he was hit with the Panic of 1893, which produced severe national depression which he was unable to reverse, ruining the Democratic Party. As a child he loved to play outdoor sports and pranks. Due to their family finances he was removed from school and was placed in a two year apprenticeship.

The 22nd President of the United States of America

&

The 24th President of the United States of America

Benjamin Harrison: was born in 1833 and died in 1901 He was from the State of Indiana and was elected President of the United States from March 4, 1889 till March 4, 1893. He was associated with the Republican Party. He served as U.S. Senator of Indiana from 1881 till 1887. Levi P. Morton was his Vice President.

He was the grandson of the ninth President William Henry Harrison who was associated with the Whig Party. There was near 48 years separating their presidencies. He was seen as a prominent attorney.

He served as a Colonel in the Union Army during the Civil War, later to be confirmed by Congress to become a Brigadier General. His administration dealt with the McKinley Tariff act which raised imports to almost fifty percent, it was intended to protect domestic industries from foreign competition.

The spending issue was a part of why the Republicans lost their re election to the Democrats and why Grover Cleveland once again became president. His Great Grandfather was Benjamin Harrison V, a Virginia Governor and signer of the Declaration of Independence. While his family may have been distinguished they were not wealthy. His father spent much of their farm money on education.

The 23rd President of the United States of America

William McKinley: was born in 1843 and died in 1901. He was from the State of Ohio He served as President of the United States from March 4, 1897 till September 14, 1901. He was associated with the Republican Party. He served two terms in office, but his second term was cut short due to his death by assassination. He held the office of Governor of Ohio prior to his presidency.

Garret Hobart served under him as Vice President from March 4, 1897 till November 21, 1899, where the office stayed vacant till March 4, 1901. On McKinley's second term he then had Theodore Roosevelt as his Vice President. In September of 1901 the Vice President took over as President due to President McKinley's death leaving the Vice Presidents office once again vacant.

He led his Nation to victory in the Spanish American War. He raised protective tariffs to promote American industry and maintained the nation on the gold standard rejecting inflationary proposals.

McKinley was the last president to serve in the Civil War. After the war he settled in Canton, Ohio and practiced law.

The 25ᵗʰ President of the United States of America

Theodore Roosevelt: was born in 1858 and died in 1919. He was from the State of New York. He served two terms as President of the United States from September 14, 1901 till March 4, 1909. He was associated with the Republican Party and was the previous Vice President moving into the Presidential office as president due to President McKinley's unexpected death. The vice presidency remained vacant through the first term until March 4 1905 when Charles W. Fairbanks would be elected into the Vice President seat.

Theodore Roosevelt often referred to as Teddy was an American Statesman, Author, Explorer, Soldier and naturalist. He operated a cattle ranch in the Dakotas. He had rode with the rough riders who were the 1st United States Calvary.

Conservation was a priority as he established new national parks, forests and monuments. He went on safari in Africa and traveled Europe. During World War I he opposed President Wilson for keeping the U.S. out the war with Germany. He is one of the faces that adorns Mount Rushmore.

He started out home schooled but had eventually made it to Harvard College. He wrote a book called *The Naval War of 1812*. He also served as Assistant Secretary of the Navy. He returned home as a war hero from the war in Cuba.

The 26th President of the United States of America

William Howard Taft: was born in 1857 to 1930. He was from the State of Ohio. He served as President of the United States from March 4, 1909 till March 4, 1913 serving just one term in office. He was associated with the Republican Party. He served prior to this office as the Secretary of War from 1904 to 1908.

His Vice President was James S. Sherman He was the last Vice President to die in office and the first Vice President to fly in a plane and the first Vice President to throw out the first pitch at a baseball game, ok back President Taft.

Taft is the only person to have presided over both the executive and legislative branches of the United States government. He served as a solicitor General of the United States along with serving as a Judge on the United States Court of Appeals for the sixth circuit.

He focused on the improvement of the Post Office, along with strengthening the Interstate Commerce Commission. The Taft family was a powerful family that practiced law, his father was a prominent Republican who served as Secretary of War and Attorney General under President Ulysses S. Grant.

The 27th President of the United States of America

Woodrow Wilson: was born in 1856 and died in 1924. He was from the State of New Jersey and served as President of the United States from March 4, 1913 till March 4, 1921 serving two terms in office. He was associated with the Democratic Party. He served prior to his presidency as Governor of New Jersey from 1911 till 1913. Thomas R. Marshal was his Vice President.

He earned a PhD in political science. He was a professor and scholar having worked in different institutions. Wilson reintroduced the spoken State of the Union which had been out of use since 1801. He was responsible for the Federal Reserve Act, Federal Trade Commission Act, the Clayton Anti Trust Act. There was also the Adamson Act which imposed an eight hour work day for the railroads adverting a strike by the railroads.

He was the first Democrat since Andrew Jackson to be elected two terms as President. During his second term in office he asked Congress to declare war. Wilson along with many Americans wanted to remain neutral, but there were many who despised the Germans, more than any other European country.

Wilson supported racial segregation, while his grandfather had published a pro tariff and anti slavery newspaper.

The 28th President of the United States of America

Warden G. Harding: was born in 1865 and died in 1923. He was from the State of Ohio. He served from March 4, 1921 till August 2, 1923. He died half way through his term in office. He was associated with the Republican Party. He served as U.S. Senator of Ohio from 1915 till 1921, at which time he became President of the United States.

Calvin Coolidge was his Vice President. President Harding though died mostly a popular president he was in the midst of the Teapot Dome Scandal which involved bribery between a member of his administration, The Secretary of Interior Albert B. Fall who had leased Navy petroleum reserves at Teapot Dome, Wyoming to private companies without competitive bidding included in the scandal was Attorney General Harry Daugherty. It was seen as the worst scandal in history till years later with the Water Gate scandal taking its place. Fall's was convicted of taking bribes from the oil companies and was the first Cabinet member to ever go to prison.

Harry F. Sinclair was one of the gentlemen that he leased to. Sinclair oil has been around a long time and is still prominent in many areas of our nation today.

President Harding's family were abolitionists He grew up learning about the newspaper industry.

The 29th President of the United States of America

Calvin Coolidge: was born in 1872 and died in 1933. He was from the State of Massachusetts. He served as the President of the United States from August 2, 1923 till March 4, 1929. He was associated with the Republican party. He was Vice President prior to taking over as President due to Harding's death.

After finishing off his first term in office he was then re elected another term. Charles G. Dawes was his Vice President during his second term, while the vice presidency remained vacant on the first term.

He was a lawyer from Vermont, he worked his way up into the Massachusetts political arena eventually becoming the Governor of Massachusetts. He restored public confidence while in office, putting the scandals of his predecessor behind them.

He was seen as having the reputation of a small town conservative. He was the fourth of five presidents to have died during the term of their direct successor. He was for smaller government, where others believed that the government should have more control in regulating our economy.

The 30th President of the United States of America

Where our Presidents are from

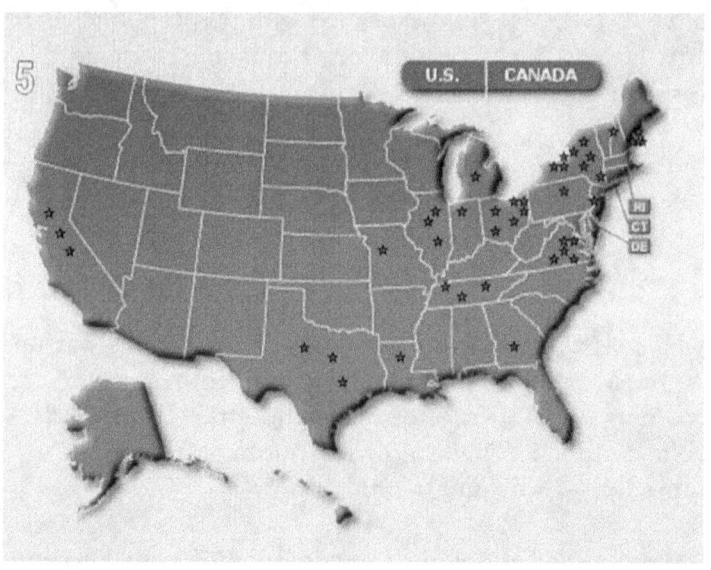

If we look at this map it shows where our Presidents have come from. Most appear to be in the Eastern time zone most appear to be also from Northern States. It also shows all the States that have never had a president covering the last 226 years. Virginia 5, Massachusetts 4, Tennessee 3, Ohio 6, New York 8, Louisiana 1, New Hampshire 1, Pennsylvania 1, Illinois 3, Indiana 1, New Jersey 1, Texas 3, California 3, Missouri 1, Arkansas 1, Georgia 1, and Michigan 1.

CHAPTER NINE

We have just gone over 72 more years Covering the time between President Abraham Lincoln up to President Calvin Coolidge. From the end of the Civil War to World War I. Before I go on think how just in your lifetime, your views and opinions have changed, so has our country's and leaders.

Remember all these presidents so far were born in the 1800s or before. Things are different today then back then, however saying that we see how there is still corruption, political parties that battle each other and conflict throughout the regions. America is still seen as a force not to take lightly.

As we cover these last 15 presidents, remember how our allies and our enemies see us today verses yesterday. Let's move on and meet our next group of presidents.

Herbert Hoover: was born in 1874 and died in 1964. He was from the State of California. He served one term in office as President of the United States from March 4, 1929 till March 4, 1933. He was associated with the Republican Party. He served as Secretary of Commerce from 1921 till 1928 prior to his presidency.

He was raised as a Quaker and was a professional mining engineer. Hoover won the Republican nomination easily, despite having no elected office experience. He was one of only two presidents, including Taft that were elected without electoral experience, or being of high ranking in the military.

8 months after being in office he was challenged with the Wall Street crash of 1929 and the great depression. He was the first president to donate his paycheck to charity as he had made a small fortune off his mining, President Kennedy was the other.

Hoover was born in West Branch Iowa only four and a half hours from where I grew up. His father was a blacksmith and farm implement store owner.

President Truman appointed Hoover to head the Hoover Commission, which was to organize the executive branch of government.

The 31st President of the United States of America

Franklin D. Roosevelt: was born in 1882 and died in 1945. He was from the State of New York and elected to serve 4 terms in the White House as President of the United States, serving from March 4, 1933 till April 12, 1945 when he died. He was associated with the Democratic Party. He served as Governor of New York from 1929 till 1932.

During his long stay in office he had three different Vice Presidents serve under him, they were John Nance Garner, Henry A Wallace and Harry S. Truman. He led our nation in a time of worldwide economic depression.

He came from a prominent family and attended the elite institutions of Groton Schools and Harvard College. He served in the New York State Senate and served as the Secretary of the Navy. Roosevelt had caught polio and his political career was put on hold a while. He then founded a treatment center for those with polio.

During his first hundred days in office he spearheaded legislation issuing an abundance of executive orders that instituted the new deal which were different programs to help with relief of the unemployed. With World War II Roosevelt brought strong diplomatic and financial support to China and the United Kingdom while remaining officially neutral Due to Japans invasion of China and by the aggression of Nazi Germany.

The 32nd President of the United States of America

Harry S. Truman: was born in 1884 and died in 1972. He was from the State of Missouri. He served two terms in office from April 12, 1945 when as Vice President he took over as President due to Roosevelt dying in office. He was then elected on the second term finishing his presidency on January 20, 1953.

Four weeks after he took office the United Nations successfully ended World War II, as tensions with the Soviet Union increased with the United States and NATO marking the start of the cold war.

Truman served the last five months of World War I in combat in France as an artillery officer in the Army National Guard.

Truman approved the use of atomic weapons against Japan, hoping to encourage Japan in to surrendering and save American lives. Truman was responsible for the Executive order 9981, which abolished racial discrimination in the military and eventually ended the segregation in the military as well.

His father had many friends that were active in the Democratic Party who help Harry gain his first political position. He was rejected from West Point due to poor eye sight and only passed in the National Guard by memorizing the eye chart the second time he took it. He was willing to fight for his country.

The 33rd President of the United States of America

Dwight D. Eisenhower: was born in 1890 and died in 1969. He was from the State of New York. He served two terms in office as President of the United States, from January 20, 1953 till January 20, 1961. He was associated with the Republican Party.

He was Supreme Allied Commander Europe, from 1949 till 1952. His Vice President was Richard Nixon. He was the last president to be born in the 19th Century. President Eisenhower was a Five Star General in the United States Army during World War II. He was responsible for planning and supervising the invasion of North Africa called Operation Torch in 1942 and 1943 along witch a successful invasion in France and Germany in 1944 and 1945. He was the first Supreme Commander of NATO.

Eisenhower's main goal was to keep pressure on the Soviet Union and to reduce the Federal deficit. After the Soviets launched their satellite program Eisenhower responded, authorizing the establishment of NASA. He expanded social security and for the most part left much of the political activity to Vice President Nixon.

Through the Atomic Energy Act he encouraged peaceful use of nuclear power.

The 34th President of the United States of America

John F. Kennedy: was born in 1917 and died in 1963. He was the first president born in the twentieth Century. He was from the State of Massachusetts. He served one term in office as President of the United States from January 20, 1961 till November 22, 1963 at which time he died by assassination. He was associated with the Democratic Party. Prior to his presidency he was a Senator from Massachusetts serving from 1953 till 1960. His Vice President was Lynden B. Johnson.

During his presidency there was the Cuban Missile Crisis, which was a confrontation between the United States and the Soviet Union over Soviet ballistic missiles deployed in Cuba it was on national TV and was the closest thing to a near nuclear war. There was the Bay of Pigs invasion, which was a failed military invasion by the CIA to take out the Democratic Revolutionary Front and over throw the communist government of Fidel Castro. There was the Nuclear Test Ban Treaty, Peace Corp and Space Race. There was the Building of the Berlin Wall.

There was the Civil Rights Movement and the increased involvement in the Vietnam War. Kennedy was assassinated in Texas by a sniper name Lee Harvey Oswald at the Texas School Book Depository, who then was assassinated by Jack Ruby.

He was the first president in my lifetime with me being born in 1962.

The 35th President of the United States of America

Lynden B. Johnson: was born in 1908 and died in 1973. He was from the State of Texas. On November 22,1963 Lynden B. Johnson took office as President of the United States, Due to President Kennedy's death by assassination. He served the remainder of Kennedy's term and was then re-elected for another four year term, ending his presidency January 20, 1969. He was associated with the Democratic Party. He served prior to his presidency as Vice President, leaving that office spot vacant the remainder of his first term while he was President.

He served as a United States Representative and as a United States Senator. He is one of only four Presidents to have served as President, Vice President, House, and Senate. As President he was for Civil Rights, Public Broadcasting and Medicare and Medicaid.

The civil rights bill signed by Johnson banned racial discrimination in public areas. The Immigration nationality Act of 1965 abolished the National Origins Formula, which had been in place since the emergency quota Act of 1921. Johnson fought the war on poverty helping those in poverty rise above. In the summer of 1965 riots broke out and crime rates soared. Johnson is ranked by some historians very positively due to his policies he saw through, such as civil rights, gun control, wilderness preservations and social security.

The 36th President of the United States of America

Richard Nixon: was born in 1913 and died in 1994. He was from the State of California He served as President of the United States from January 20, 1969 till August 9, 1974. He was associated with the Republican Party and served as Vice President from 1953 till 1961.

He is the only United States President that has ever resigned in office. He had previously served as a Representative and Senator from California. Nixon ended the involvement in the Vietnam War and ended the draft as well. Nixon's visit to the Peoples Republic of China opened diplomatic relations between the two nations.

Nixon initiated the Anti ballistic missile treaty with the Soviet Union. He enforced desegregation and created the Environmental Protection Agency. He presided over the Apollo 11 moon landing.

Then there was the scandal of the century, known as Water Gate, which forced him to resign or most likely be Impeached. It was over array of things from wire tapping, bugging officials to harassment using the FBI, CIA, and IRS to intimidate, a blatant abuse of power.

The 37th President of the United States of America

Gerald Ford: was born in 1913 and died in 2006. He was from the State of Michigan. He served one term in office as the President of the United States from August 9, 1974 till January 20, 1977. He was associated with the Republican Party. He served as Vice President from December 6, 1973 till August 9, 1974. His Vice President was Nelson Rockefeller.

He was the first person appointed to the Vice presidency under the 25th Amendment following the resignation of Vice President Spiro Agnew. To date he is the first and only person to become President and Vice President without being elected into office.

Ford had served 13 terms as Representative from Michigan's 5th Congressional district. Ford presided over the worst economy in the four decades since the Great Depression.

Ford had lived longer than any other U.S. President and served the shortest term in office from any of the Presidents before him that did not die in office.

Ford was involved in Boy Scouts of America and earned the highest award of Eagle Scout. It was an important part of his life and at his funeral 400 Eagle Scouts attended and were part of the procession.

The 38th President of the United States of America.

Jimmy Carter: was born in 1924. He is from the State of Georgia He served one term as President of the United States from January 20, 1977 till January 20, 1981. He was associated with the Democratic Party. Prior to his presidency he was Governor of Georgia from 1971 till 1975. Walter Mondale was his Vice President.

He is an author, along with being awarded the Nobel Peace Prize for his work with the Carter Foundation. Jimmy Carter was a peanut farmer that served two terms as Georgia State Senator and one term as Governor of Georgia.

On his second day in the presidency he pardoned all evaders of the Vietnam War draft. During Carter's term in office he created two new cabinet level departments, the Department of Energy and Department of Education. He pursued the Panama Canal treaties returning the canal back to Panama.

During his term in office he was confronted with the Iran hostage crisis, the 1979 energy crisis, The Three Mile Island Nuclear accident and the Soviet invasion of Afghanistan. Carter is a supporter of President Obama, but is critical of his foreign policies and of not closing down Guantanamo Bay detention camp.

The 39th President of the United States of America

Ronald Reagan: was born in 1911 and died in 2004. He was from the State of California. He served two terms in office as the President of the United States from January 20, 1981 till January 20, 1989. He was associated with the Republican Party He served prior to his presidency as the Governor of California. George H. W. Busch was his Vice President.

He was an American politician and an actor. He was raised in a poor family in a small town in Illinois. He also worked as a sports announcer on several regional radio stations. He fought against communism. He had started off as a Liberal Democrat and then changed to become a Conservative Republican.

He introduced Reaganomics advocating tax rate reductions to spur economic growth. He saw to a reduction of government spending. He fought a war against drugs, he survived an assassination attempt on his life by John Hinckley Jr. James Brady was wounded protecting the President and later had a Bill named the Brady Bill named after him There was the Iran Contra Affair where Arms were sold secretly to Iran by senior Administration officials in Reagan's second term in office. It was an attempt to get back seven American hostages being held in Lebanon. The Reagan administration interfered seeing that important documents ended up getting destroyed.

He told the Soviet Leader Mikhail Gorbachev to Tear down this wall referring to the Berlin Wall. Which was torn down.

The 40th President of the United States of America

George W. H. Busch: was born in 1924. He is from the State of Texas. He has served one term in office from January 20, 1989 till January 20, 1993. He was associated with the Republican Party. He served as Vice President prior to his presidency. His Vice President was Dan Quayle.

President Busch previously served as a Congressman and was the Director of the Central Intelligence, commonly known as the CIA. He is also the last living former President who is a Veteran of World War II. His father Prescott Busch was a Senator as well.

He postponed his college and enlisted in the United States Navy following the attack on Pearl Harbor. He was the youngest aviator in the U.S. Navy at the time. Upon the end of the war he attended Yale University and went into the oil business becoming a millionaire at age 40.

As President oversaw the operations in the Persian Gulf Desert Shield and Desert Storm. The war was watched on national television networks like CNN Americans for the first time could witness the battles live on TV.
Other coalitions joined the battle making it the largest military alliance since World War II.

The 41st President of the United States of America

Bill Clinton: was born in 1946. He was from the State of Arkansas. He served two terms in office as President of the United States of America. He is associated with the Democratic Party. He was Governor of Arkansas from 1979 to 1981 and from 1983 to 1992. His Vice President was Al Gore.

He had previously been a States Attorney General. He is Married to Hillary Clinton who was former Secretary of State and currently under scrutiny with the Benghazi attack and her Email scandal where thousand and thousand of emails have temporarily have disappeared, putting our national security at risk. Let's get back to Bill.

He was the third youngest President and the first from the baby boomers generation. He signed into law the North America Free Trade Agreement, this was between Canada , Mexico and the United States The AFL-CIO blames the loss of 700,000 manufacturing jobs sent to Mexico over the trade agreement. He passed health care reform and Children health insurance program. He too was not without scandal as he was investigated and impeached on obstruction of justice in the Monica Lewinsky scandal, which involved inappropriate sexual misconduct. He was acquitted by the U.S. Senate.

The 42nd President of the United States of America

George W. Busch: was born in 1946. He is from the State of Texas. He served two terms as President of the United States from January 20, 2001 till January 20, 2009. He was associated with the Republican Party. He was Governor of Texas from 1995 till 2000. His Vice President was Dick Cheney.

He graduated from Yale University in 1968 and then from Harvard Business school in 1975. He at one time co-owned the Texas Rangers baseball team. He is the second President to be the son of a former President. He is Jeb Busch's brother, who is currently running for the 2016 Presidential election on the Republican side.

During his term in office on September 11, 2001America comes under attack by terrorists from within our borders. The United States goes to war and we eventually capture Saddam Hussein who later is executed. We take on other terrorist organizations such as Al-Qaida. He promoted policies on the economy, healthcare, broad tax cuts, the Patriot Act, No Child Left Behind Act. There was Hurricane Katrina which hurt New Orleans, Louisiana.

In 2007 The United States entered its longest post-World War II recession since the great recession.

The 43rd President of the United States of America

Barack Obama: was born in 1961 He is from the State of Illinois. He is currently serving his second term in office as the President of the United States. He is associated with the Democratic Party. He served from 2005 till 2008 as U.S. Senator of Illinois. His Vice President is Joe Biden.

He is considered the first African American to hold the office of the President of the United States. He is also the first President to not show his birth certificate showing his eligibility to be president in the first place. Obama Beat out his Democratic adversary Hillary Rodham Clinton in 2008.

While in office he put in place the Patient Protection and Affordable Care Act, commonly known as Obama Care. We all know this has failed miserably. Obama has divided our country by race, by lawlessness and by wealth. He has sat back and watch communities get destroyed as he encouraged rioters to vent inappropriately. He has abused his powers as he tries to use Executive orders to manipulate the American people.

Obama ended the War in Iraq only to now have Isis. He fought gun control using the Sandy Hook Elementary school shooting that has been seen as questionable or faked. He normalized U.S. relations with Cuba however Congress has not approved the lift on the embargo. Let's not forget the Iranian Nuclear deal he put in place giving America nothing again not following true protocol.

The 44th President of the United States of America

We have just covered all 44 presidents of the United States, with George Washington being the first back in 1789, 226 years ago. We are now in the midst of a new president as the Republicans and Democrats battle among each other. Some things that might appear interesting are that most the presidents lived in the eastern Time zone. If you follow the Democrats and the Republicans you will see that they keep switching every 4 to 8 years and a few 12 year term extensions as well. This is one of the reasons many of Americans are so upset, the party may switch but nothing gets accomplished.

If we check when our military is at its weakest it seems to be due to the Democratic years when cutting back on our military along with higher unemployment, which is when they are constantly creating new programs or more handouts. Just my opinion on these notes.

If we think about the 226 years that our Country has been led by just 44 presidents, or less if we group them in families like the Busch's, Adams's, Roosevelt's.

Americans are tired of being lied to, used and forgotten, controlled and manipulated. I hope the next President will represent all of us and unite us once again as a great nation.

CHAPTER TEN

It is time to look at who we should pick for President. I think it is important to look at everything and everyone. I will say that we just got done last night listening to CNBC mediate the Republican Presidential debate and they were totally unprofessional and bias. They tried to attack all the presidential candidates on the Republican side.

It was just this last week that one of the Committees questioned Hillary Rodham Clinton in regards to her position as Secretary of State during the Benghazi crisis and her being dishonest and lying to the American people. It was proven she lied, yet her Democratic constituents tried to minimize her behaviors and justify her actions. This is a perfect example of why Americans are tired of the politics and political parties that think they are above the law.

Let the next President be an American rather than a Party.

I have decided that I am Voting for the one candidate that has been himself from the beginning. Is he rich and should that matter? Most the Presidents before came from wealth from owning plantations and slaves to oil companies. Most of our President seemed to have gotten law degrees or studied at a prestigious college. While some did come from poor families it is the honesty, integrity, and transparency Americans want. We want to know what's going on in the White House. We want others to respect us and our nation again. We want our children to live safely and have bright futures.

I will at this time definitely not vote for a Democrat like Bernie Sanders who is a socialist. I will not Vote for Hillary Clinton who is a liar and everything she touches turns to stone. How can leaders of other countries trust anything she says when she lies to her own people?

If we look at the Republican side there are a lot to choose from, but it is picking the best one we desire. I want a president that is going to be about America not about being Republican or Democrat.

I want a president that follows through with what he says and supports our local law enforcement agencies. I want to hold the terrorist accountable for their actions and call them what they are. I want a president that says all lives matter black and white, or just keep it simple all American lives.

I will tell you who I want and why, but your decision must be your decision but at least look at what this book has covered.

Donald Trump

Is my choice for President. He says what he thinks and means what he says.

Sure Donald is flamboyant, he is exciting and entertaining. He is a proud American that has had enough. He has brought up issues that others would rather avoid, such as illegal immigration. He has a plan on the economy, along with key advisors to assist. He has been challenged on his bankruptcy history. Donald has been up front and honest, not trying to hide or minimize He has definitely taken advantage of loop holes, he'll tell you so, but following the law to the letter.

Why not use his knowledge and wisdom to make America strong and start weeding out politicians and put in true representatives, there to represent us and not them. Let's see what the King of Saudi Arabia does when Mr. Trump looks him in the eyes rather than bow at his feet like Obama did. Let's ask Mr. Trump what his comments would be on those that wish to riot and loot to express their opinions.

We could ask the military who they would wish to be their Commander in Chief, one who will build a strong military and strong communities. Let us not hate Mr. Trump for being rich, for it is everyone's dream to strike it rich. For those that are not rich, should we not worry they will be tempted by wealth from the Lobbyists?

Which Presidential candidate has remained himself and not swayed his words to fit the moment, Donald Trump.

Remember what people used to think about Ronald Reagan. I see a lot of similarities. They can challenge him on lack of knowledge or experience in government, but the truth is what tasks he is given seems to get completed almost like Celebrity Apprentice.

This book is full of history and facts, it's full of presidential candidates promises and goals. Read this book and watch the news. History is what others have made it, but the future is what we make it.

ABOUT THE AUTHOR

Timothy J. Amdahl grew up in a small town, called Estherville, Iowa. He graduated in 1981 and served two years with the Army and then transferred in to the United States Marine Corps. He was honorably discharged in 1987 after serving four and a half years in the Marine Corps. He has worked as a youth counselor for four years helping the children of our future.

He is married with four children and is currently working for the Illinois Department of Corrections as a Correctional officer, having already served fourteen years. He is a proud American who only wishes to unite our country once again in these troubling times.

Changing America is focused on bringing out concerns and challenging all of us on keeping our government honest and Americans safe with the hope our country can once again prosper. You need me and I need you, let's make America great again Let us pick the next President of the United States.

www.ingramcontent.com/pod-product-compliance
Lightning Source LLC
Chambersburg PA
CBHW071339280526
45787CB00001B/152